FORWARD/COMMENTARY

The National Institute of Standards and Technology (NIST) is a measurement standards laboratory, and a non-regulatory agency of the United States Department of Commerce. Its mission is to promote innovation and industrial competitiveness. Founded in 1901, as the National Bureau of Standards, NIST was formed with the mandate to provide standard weights and measures, and to serve as the national physical laboratory for the United States. With a world-class measurement and testing laboratory encompassing a wide range of areas of computer science, mathematics, statistics, and systems engineering, NIST's cybersecurity program supports its overall mission to promote U.S. innovation and industrial competitiveness by advancing measurement science, standards, and related technology through research and development in ways that enhance economic security and improve our quality of life.

The need for cybersecurity standards and best practices that address interoperability, usability and privacy has been shown to be critical for the nation. NIST's cybersecurity programs seek to enable greater development and application of practical, innovative security technologies and methodologies that enhance the country's ability to address current and future computer and information security challenges.

The cybersecurity publications produced by NIST cover a wide range of cybersecurity concepts that are carefully designed to work together to produce a holistic approach to cybersecurity primarily for government agencies and constitute the best practices used by industry. This holistic strategy to cybersecurity covers the gamut of security subjects from development of secure encryption standards for communication and storage of information while at rest to how best to recover from a cyber-attack.

Why buy a book you can download for free?

Some are available only in electronic media. Some online docs are missing pages or barely legible.

We at 4th Watch Books are former government employees, so we know how government employees actually use the standards. When a new standard is released, an engineer prints it out, punches holes and puts it in a 3-ring binder. While this is not a big deal for a 5 or 10-page document, many NIST documents are over 100 pages and printing a large document is a time-consuming effort. So, an engineer that's paid $75 an hour is spending hours simply printing out the tools needed to do the job. That's time that could be better spent doing engineering. We publish these documents so engineers can focus on what they were hired to do – engineering. It's much more cost-effective to just order the latest version from Amazon.com

If there is a standard you would like published, let us know. Our web site is Cybah.webplus.net

CyberSecurity Standards Library™

Get a Complete Library of Over 300 Cybersecurity Standards on 1 Convenient DVD!

The **4th Watch CyberSecurity Standards Library** is a DVD disc that puts over 300 current and archived cybersecurity standards from NIST, DOD, DHS, CNSS and NERC at your fingertips! Many of these cybersecurity standards are hard to find and we included the current version and a previous version for many of them. The DVD includes four books written by Luis Ayala: **The Cyber Dictionary, Cybersecurity Standards, Cyber-Security Glossary of Building Hacks and Cyber-Attacks**, and **Cyber-Physical Attack Defenses: Preventing Damage to Buildings and Utilities**.

- ✓ DVD includes many Hard-to-find Cybersecurity Standards - some still in Draft.
- ✓ Docs are organized by source and listed numerically so each standard is easy to locate.
- ✓ The listing of standards on the DVD includes an abstract of the subject, and date issued.
- ✓ PDF format for use on PC, Mac, eReaders, or tablets.
- ✓ No need for WiFi / Internet.
- ✓ Save countless hours of searching and downloading.
- ✓ Carry in a briefcase - terrific for travel.

4th Watch Publishing is releasing the CyberSecurity Standards Library DVD to make it easier for you to access the tools you need to ensure the security of your computer networks and SCADA systems. We also publish many of these standards on demand so you don't need to waste valuable time searching for the latest version of a standard, printing hundreds of pages and punching holes so they can go in a three-ring binder. **Order on Amazon.com**

The DVD works on PC and Mac with the standards in PDF format. To view the CyberSecurity Standards Library on the DVD, a computer with a DVD drive is required. The most current version of your internet browser, at least 2GB of RAM, and current version of Adobe Reader is recommended. (Compatible browsers include Internet Explorer 8+, Mozilla Firefox 4+, Apple Safari 5+, Google Chrome 15+)

Interagency Report 7316

NIST

**National Institute of
Standards and Technology**
Technology Administration
U.S. Department of Commerce

Assessment of
Access Control Systems

Vincent C. Hu
David F. Ferraiolo
D. Rick Kuhn

Interagency Report 7316

Assessment of Access Control Systems

Vincent C. Hu
David F. Ferraiolo
D. Rick Kuhn

COMPUTER SECURITY

Computer Security Division
Information Technology Laboratory
National Institute of Standards and Technology
Gaithersburg, MD 20899-8930

September 2006

U.S. Department of Commerce

Carlos M. Gutierrez, Secretary

Technology Administration

Robert C. Cresanti, Under Secretary of Commerce for Technology

National Institute of Standards and Technology

William Jeffrey, Director

Reports on Computer Systems Technology

The Information Technology Laboratory (ITL) at the National Institute of Standards and Technology (NIST) promotes the U.S. economy and public welfare by providing technical leadership for the Nation's measurement and standards infrastructure. ITL develops tests, test methods, reference data, proof of concept implementations, and technical analyses to advance the development and productive use of information technology. ITL's responsibilities include the development of technical, physical, administrative, and management standards and guidelines for the cost-effective security and privacy of sensitive unclassified information in federal computer systems. This Interagency Report discusses ITL's research, guidance, and outreach efforts in computer security, and its collaborative activities with industry, government, and academic organizations.

**National Institute of Standards and Technology Interagency Report 7316,
60 pages (September 2006)**

Abstract

Adequate security of information and information systems is a fundamental management responsibility. Nearly all applications that deal with financial, privacy, safety, or defense include some form of access control. Access control is concerned with determining the allowed activities of legitimate users, mediating every attempt by a user to access a resource in the system. In some systems, complete access is granted after successful authentication of the user, but most systems require more sophisticated and complex control. In addition to the *authentication* mechanism (such as a password), access control is concerned with how *authorizations* are structured. In some cases, authorization may mirror the structure of the organization, while in others it may be based on the sensitivity level of various documents and the clearance level of the user accessing those documents. This publication explains some of the commonly used access control services available in information technology systems.

Organizations planning to implement an access control system should consider three abstractions: access control policies, models, and mechanisms. Access control *policies* are high-level requirements that specify how access is managed and who may access information under what circumstances. For instance, policies may pertain to resource usage within or across organizational units or may be based on need-to-know, competence, authority, obligation, or conflict-of-interest factors. At a high level, access control policies are enforced through a *mechanism* that translates a user's access request, often in terms of a structure that a system provides. An access control list is a familiar example of an access control mechanism. Access control *models* bridge the gap in abstraction between policy and mechanism. Rather than attempting to evaluate and analyze access control systems exclusively at the mechanism level, security models are usually written to describe the security properties of an access control system. Security models are formal presentations of the security policy enforced by the system and are useful for proving theoretical limitations of a system. Discretionary access control, which allows the creator of a file to delegate access to others, is one of the simplest examples of a model.

As systems grow in size and complexity, access control is a special concern for systems that are distributed across multiple computers. These *distributed systems* can be a formidable challenge for developers, because they may use a variety of access control mechanisms that must be integrated to support the organization's policy; for example, role-based access control that can enforce administrator-specified rules is often used. Popular database management system designs, such as Structured Query Language (SQL), incorporate many aspects of role- and rule-based access. Services that are particularly useful in implementing distributed access control include the Lightweight Directory Access Protocol (LDAP), capability-based Kerberos, and the Extensible Markup Language (XML)-based Extensible Access Control Markup Language (XACML).

A state of access control is said to be safe if no permission can be leaked to an unauthorized or uninvited principal. To assure the safety of an access control system, it is essential to make certain that the access control configuration (e.g., access control model) will not result in the leakage of permissions to an unauthorized principal. Even though the general safety computation is proven undecidable [HRU76], practical mechanisms exist for achieving the safety requirement, such as safety constraints built into the mechanism.

Access control systems come with a wide variety of features and administrative capabilities, and the operational impact can be significant. In particular, this impact can pertain to administrative and user productivity, as well as to the organization's ability to perform its mission. Therefore, it is reasonable to use a quality metric to verify the administrative capabilities, administrative cost, policy coverage, extensibility, and performance qualities of access control systems.

Appendix C summarizes mechanisms and models supported by popular platforms such as Microsoft Windows, UNIX/Linux, and SQL database management systems.

Acknowledgements

The authors wish to thank their colleagues who reviewed drafts of this document, including Karen Kent, Shirley Radack, Wayne Jansen, Tim Grance, and Tom Karygiannis. The authors also gratefully acknowledge and appreciate the comments and contributions made by government agencies, private organizations, and individuals in providing direction and assistance in the development of this document.

TABLE OF CONTENTS

TABLE OF FIGURES

TABLE OF TABLES

1   INTRODUCTION

1.1   Authority

The National Institute of Standards and Technology (NIST) developed this document in furtherance of its statutory responsibilities under the Federal Information Security Management Act (FISMA) of 2002, Public Law 107-347.

NIST is responsible for developing standards and guidelines, including minimum requirements, for providing adequate information security for all agency operations and assets, but such standards and guidelines shall not apply to national security systems. This document is consistent with the requirements of the Office of Management and Budget (OMB) Circular A-130, Section 8b(3), "Securing Agency Information Systems," as analyzed in A-130, Appendix IV: Analysis of Key Sections. Supplemental information is provided in A-130, Appendix III.

This guideline has been prepared for use by federal agencies. It may be used by nongovernmental organizations on a voluntary basis and is not subject to copyright, though attribution is desired.

Nothing in this document should be taken to contradict standards and guidelines made mandatory and binding on federal agencies by the Secretary of Commerce under statutory authority, nor should these guidelines be interpreted as altering or superseding the existing authorities of the Secretary of Commerce, Director of the OMB, or any other federal official.

1.2   Document Scope and Purpose

The purpose of this document is to provide agencies with background information on access control policies, models, and mechanisms to assist them in securing their computer applications. The document discusses the capabilities, limitations, and qualities of the access control mechanisms that are embedded for each access control policy.

1.3   Audience and Assumptions

This document is intended to provide practical and conceptual guidance for security managers, administrators, and procurement officers whose expertise is related to access control. The authors assume that the readers have basic operating system, database, and networking expertise, as well as some security expertise, especially in the field of access control. Because of the constantly changing nature of the information technology industry, readers are strongly encouraged to take advantage of other resources (including those listed in this document) for more current and detailed information.

1.4   Document Organization

This document is divided into seven sections, followed by three appendixes. Section 1 states the authority, scope, purpose, audience, and assumptions of this document. Section 2 introduces the terminology that is widely used in the field of access control and basic abstractions of controls: access control policies, models, and mechanisms. Section 2 also introduces major access control policies; popular policies are provided with the discussions. The focus of this document is presented in Section 3, which introduces some popular access control mechanisms and presents their advantages and limitations, along with examples. Section 4 is devoted to the broader applications of access control mechanisms for distributed systems. Section 5 discusses the safety issues of access control systems. Section 6 lists and explains some measurements for the quality of an access control mechanism. Section 7 presents the conclusion to the document. Appendixes A - Glossary, B - Acronyms, C - Commercial Access Control Systems, and References provide information that supports the document.

2 OVERVIEW OF ACCESS CONTROL

This section introduces concepts, common terms, and basic (popular) policies and models of access control. The contents of this section are referenced throughout the document.

Access control is concerned with determining the allowed activities of legitimate users, mediating every attempt by a user to access a resource in the system. A given information technology (IT) infrastructure can implement access control systems in many places and at different levels. Operating systems use access control to protect files and directories. Database management systems DBMS apply access control to regulate access to tables and views. Most commercially available application systems implement access control, often independent of the operating systems and/or DBMSs on which they are installed.

The objectives of an access control system are often described in terms of protecting system resources against inappropriate or undesired user access. From a business perspective, this objective could just as well be described in terms of the optimal sharing of information. After all, the main objective of IT is to make information available to users and applications. A greater degree of sharing may get in the way of resource protection; in reality, a well-managed and effective access control system actually facilitates sharing. A sufficiently fine-grained access control mechanism can enable selective sharing of information where in its absence, sharing may be considered too risky altogether [FKC03].

2.1 Concepts

This section introduces some of the concepts that are commonly used in the access control research community and are also used throughout this document.

- **Object:** An entity that contains or receives information. Access to an object potentially implies access to the information it contains. Examples of objects are records, fields (in a database record), blocks, pages, segments, files, directories, directory trees, process, and programs, as well as processors, video displays, keyboards, clocks, printers, and network nodes. Devices such as electrical switches, disc drives, relays, and mechanical components connected to a computer system may also be included in the category of objects [NCSC88].
- **Subject:** An active entity, generally in the form of a person, process, or device that causes information to flow among objects (see below) or changes the system state [NCSC88].
- **Operation:** An active process invoked by a subject; for example, when an automatic teller machine (ATM) user enters a card and correct personal identification number (PIN), the control program operation on the user's behalf is a process, but the subject can initiate more than one operation-deposit, withdrawal, balance inquiry, etc. [FKC03]
- **Permission (privilege):** An authorization to perform some action on the system. In most computer security literature, the term *permission* refers to some combination of object and operation. A particular operation used on two different objects represents two distinct permissions, and similarly, two different operations applied to a single object represent two distinct permissions. For example, a bank teller may have permissions to execute debit and credit operations on customer records through transactions, while an accountant may

execute debit and credit operations on the general ledger, which consolidates the bank's accounting data [FKC03].

- **Access Control List (ACL):** A list associated with an object that specifies all the subjects that can access the object, along with their rights to the object. Each entry in the list is a pair (subject, set of rights). An ACL corresponds to a column of the access control matrix (described next). ACLs are frequently implemented directly or as an approximation in modern operating systems.

- **Access Control Matrix:** A table in which each row represents a subject, each column represents an object, and each entry is the set of access rights for that subject to that object. In general, the access control matrix is sparse: most subjects do not have access rights to most objects. Therefore, different representations have been proposed. The access control matrix can be represented as a list of triples, having the form <subject, rights, object>. Searching a large number of these triples is inefficient enough that this implementation is seldom used [Sum97]. Rather, the matrix is typically subdivided into columns (ACLs) or rows (capabilities).

- **Separation of Duty (SOD):** The principle that no user should be given enough privileges to misuse the system. For example, the person authorizing a paycheck should not also be the one who can prepare it. Separation of duties can be enforced either *statically* by defining conflicting roles (i.e., roles which cannot be executed by the same user) or *dynamically* by enforcing the control at access time. An example of dynamic separation of duty is the two-person rule. The first user to execute a two-person operation can be any authorized user, whereas the second user can be any authorized user different from the first. There are various types of SOD; an important one is a *history-based* SOD that regulates, for example, that the same subject (role) cannot access the same object a certain number of times.

- **Safety:** Measures that the access control configuration (e.g., access control mechanism or model) will not result in the leakage of permissions to an unauthorized principal. Thus, a configuration is said to be safe if no permission can be leaked to an unauthorized or unintended principal.

- **Domain and Type Enforcement:** The grouping of processes into domains, and objects into types, such that access operations (such as read, write, execute, and create) are restricted from domains to types and between domains. A process belongs to one domain at any given time and transits to other domains by sending signals or executing a file in a new domain [BSS95].

2.2   Policies, Models, and Mechanisms

When planning an access control system, three abstractions of controls should be considered: access control policies, models, and mechanisms. Access control *policies* are high-level requirements that specify how access is managed and who, under what circumstances, may access what information. While access control policies can be application-specific and thus taken into consideration by the application vendor, policies are just as likely to pertain to user actions within the context of an organizational unit or across organizational boundaries. For instance, policies may pertain to resource usage within or across organizational units or may be based on need-to-know, competence, authority, obligation, or conflict-of-interest factors. Such policies may span multiple computing platforms and applications.

At a high level, access control policies are enforced through a *mechanism* that translates a user's access request, often in terms of a structure that a system provides. There are a wide variety of structures; for example, a simple table lookup can be performed to grant or deny access. Although no well-accepted standard yet exists for determining their policy support, some access control mechanisms are direct implementations of formal access control policy concepts [FKC03].

Rather than attempting to evaluate and analyze access control systems exclusively at the mechanism level, security models are usually written to describe the security properties of an access control system. A *model* is a formal presentation of the security policy enforced by the system and is useful for proving theoretical limitations of a system. Access control models are of general interest to both users and vendors. They bridge the rather wide gap in abstraction between policy and mechanism. Access control mechanisms can be designed to adhere to the properties of the model. Users see an access control model as an unambiguous and precise expression of requirements. Vendors and system developers see access control models as design and implementation requirements. On one extreme, an access control model may be rigid in its implementation of a single policy. On the other extreme, a security model will allow for the expression and enforcement of a wide variety of policies and policy classes [FKC03, HFF01]. As stated previously, the focus of this document is on the practical side of the access control system; detailed descriptions of access control models are not included in this publication [NCSC91].

This section provides additional information on access control policies and gives examples of several types of policies. Section 2.2.2.2 introduces the concept of role-based access control. Finally, Section 2.2.2.3 discusses the type and use of temporal constraints in access control policies.

Generating a list of access control policies is of limited value, since business objectives, tolerance for risk, corporate culture, and the regulatory responsibilities that influence policy differ from enterprise to enterprise, and even from organizational unit to organizational unit. The access control policies within a hospital may pertain to privacy and competency (e.g., only doctors and nurse practitioners may prescribe medication), and hospital policies will differ greatly from those of a military system or a financial institution. Even within a specific business domain, policy will differ from institution to institution. Furthermore, access control policies are dynamic in nature, in that they are likely to change over time in reflection of ever-evolving business factors, government regulations, and environmental conditions. There are several well-known access control policies, which can be categorized as discretionary or non-discretionary. Typically, discretionary access control policies are associated with identity-based access control, and non-discretionary access controls are associated with rule-based controls (for example, mandatory security policy).

2.2.1   Discretionary Access Control (DAC)

DAC leaves a certain amount of access control to the discretion of the object's owner or anyone else who is authorized to control the object's access [NCSC87]. For example, it is generally used to limit a user's access to a file [NSP94]; it is the owner of the file who controls other users' accesses to the file. Only those users specified by the owner may have some combination of read, write, execute, and other permissions to the file. DAC policy tends to be very flexible and is widely used in the commercial and government sectors. However, DAC is known to be inherently weak for two reasons. First, granting read access is transitive; for example, when Ann grants Bob read access to a file, nothing stops Bob from copying the contents of Ann's file to an object that Bob controls. Bob may now grant any other user access to the copy of Ann's file without Ann's knowledge. Second, DAC policy is vulnerable to Trojan horse attacks. Because programs inherit the identity of the invoking user, Bob may, for example, write a program for Ann that, on the surface, performs some useful function, while at the same time destroys the contents of Ann's files. When investigating the problem, the audit files would indicate that Ann destroyed her own files. Thus, formally, the drawbacks of DAC are as follows:

- Information can be copied from one object to another; therefore, there is no real assurance on the flow of information in a system.
- No restrictions apply to the usage of information when the user has received it.
- The privileges for accessing objects are decided by the owner of the object, rather than through a system-wide policy that reflects the organization's security requirements.

ACLs and owner/group/other access control mechanisms are by far the most common mechanism for implementing DAC policies [FCK03]. Other mechanisms, even though not designed with DAC in mind, may have the capabilities to implement a DAC policy.

2.2.2   Non-Discretionary Access Control

In general, all access control policies other than DAC are grouped in the category of *non-discretionary access control (NDAC)*. As the name implies, policies in this category have rules that are not established at the discretion of the user. Non-discretionary policies establish controls that cannot be changed by users, but only through administrative action.

Separation of duty (SOD) policy can be used to enforce constraints on the assignment of users to roles or tasks. An example of such a static constraint is the requirement that two roles be mutually exclusive; if one role requests expenditures and another approves them, the organization may prohibit the same user from being assigned to both roles. So, membership in one role may prevent the user from being a member of one or more other roles, depending on the SOD rules, such as Work Flow [AH96] and Role-Based Access Control (see the following sections). Another example is a history-based SOD policy that regulates, for example, whether the same subject (role) can access the same object a certain number of times [SZ97]. Three popular non-discretionary access control policies are discussed in this section.

2.2.2.1   Mandatory access control (MAC)

Mandatory access control (MAC) policy means that access control policy decisions are made by a central authority, not by the individual owner of an object, and the owner cannot change access rights. An example of MAC occurs in military security, where an individual data owner does not decide who has a *Top Secret* clearance, nor can the owner change the classification of an object from *Top Secret* to *Secret* [Pfl97]. MAC is the most mentioned NDAC policy.

The need for a MAC mechanism arises when the security policy of a system dictates that:

1. Protection decisions must not be decided by the object owner.
2. The system must enforce the protection decisions (i.e., the system enforces the security policy over the wishes or intentions of the object owner).

Usually a labeling mechanism and a set of interfaces are used to determine access based on the MAC policy; for example, a user who is running a process at the *Secret* classification should not be allowed to read a file with a label of *Top Secret*. This is known as the "simple security rule," or "no read up." Conversely, a user who is running a process with a label of *Secret* should not be allowed to write to a file with a label of *Confidential*. This rule is called the "*-property" (pronounced "star property") or "no write down." The *-property is required to maintain system security in an automated environment. A variation on this rule called the "strict *-property" requires that information can be written at, but not above, the subject's clearance level. Multilevel security models such as the Bell-La Padula Confidentiality and Biba Integrity models are used to formally specify this kind of MAC policy. However, information can pass through a covert channel in MAC, where information of a higher security class is deduced by inference such as assembling and intelligently combining information of a lower security class. Popular mechanisms used in implementing MAC policies are demonstrated in Section 3.

2.2.2.2   Role-based access control

Although RBAC is technically a form of non-discretionary access control [Ram02, Shi02], recent computer security texts often list RBAC as one of the three primary access control policies (the others are DAC and MAC). In RBAC, access decisions are based on the roles that individual users have as part of an organization. Users take on assigned roles (such as doctor, nurse, teller, or manager). Access rights are grouped by role name, and the use of resources is restricted to individuals authorized to assume the associated role. For example, within a hospital system, the role of doctor can include operations to perform a diagnosis, prescribe medication, and order laboratory tests; the role of researcher can be limited to gathering anonymous clinical information for studies. The use of roles to control access can be an effective means for developing and enforcing enterprise-specific security policies and for streamlining the security management process.

Under RBAC, users are granted membership into roles based on their competencies and responsibilities in the organization. The operations that a user is permitted to perform are based on the user's role. User membership into roles can be revoked easily and new memberships established as job assignments dictate. Role associations can be established when new operations are instituted, and old operations can be deleted as organizational functions change and evolve. This simplifies the administration and management of privileges; roles can be updated without updating the privileges for every user on an individual basis.

When a user is associated with a role, the user can be given no more privilege than is necessary to perform the job; since many of the responsibilities overlap between job categories, maximum privilege for each job category could cause unauthorized access. This concept of *least privilege* requires identifying the user's job functions, determining the minimum set of privileges required to perform those functions, and restricting the user to a domain with those privileges and nothing more. In less precisely controlled systems, *least privilege* is often difficult or costly to achieve because it is difficult to tailor access based on various attributes or constraints. Role hierarchies can be established to provide for the natural structure of an enterprise. A role hierarchy defines roles that have unique attributes and that may contain other roles; that is, one role may implicitly include the operations that are associated with another role.

2.2.2.3 Temporal constraints

Temporal constraints are formal statements of access policies that involve time-based restrictions on access to resources; they are required in several application scenarios. In some applications, temporal constraints may be required to limit resource use. In other types of applications, they may be required for controlling time-sensitive activities. It is these time-based constraints (in addition to other constraints like workflow precedence relationships) that must be evaluated for generating dynamic authorizations during workflow execution time. Temporal constraints may also be required in non workflow environments as well. For example, in a commercial banking enterprise, an employee should be able to assume the role of a teller (to perform transactions on customer accounts) only during designated banking hours (such as 9 a.m. to 2 p.m., Monday through Friday, and 9 a.m. to 12 p.m. on Saturday). To meet this requirement, it is necessary to specify temporal constraints that limit role availability and activation capability only to those designated banking hours.

Popular access control policies related to temporal constraints are the history-based access control policies, which are not supported by any standard access control mechanism but have practical application in many business operations such as task transactions and separation of conflicts-of-interests. *History-based access control* is defined in terms of subjects and events where the events of the system are specified as the object access operations associated with activity at a particular security level. This assures that the security policy is defined in terms of the sequence of events over time, and that the security policy decides which events of the system are permitted to ensure that information does not "flow" in an unauthorized manner. Popular history-based access control policies are Workflow and Chinese Wall, which are described below.

Workflow

Based on the definition provided by the Workflow Management Coalition (WFMC), an international organization of workflow vendors, users, and research groups, a *workflow* is a representation of an organizational or business process in which "...documents, information, or tasks are passed from one participant to another in a way that is governed by rules or procedures." A workflow separates the various activities of a given organizational process into a set of well-defined tasks. Hence, typically, a workflow (often synonymous with a process) is specified as a set of tasks and a set of dependencies among the tasks, and the sequencing of these tasks is important. The various tasks in a workflow are usually carried out by several users in accordance with organizational rules relevant to the process represented by the workflow.

The representation of a business process using a workflow involves a number of organizational rules or policies. An important class of organization policies is the organization's security policies. Within the realm of security policies, access control policies play a key role, and hence defining and enforcing access control requirements becomes a key function of a Workflow Management System (WFMS).

Figure 1 presents a schematic diagram of the overall architecture of a WFMS, which consist of two main components: design-time and run-time. The design-time component consists of a set of tools (called the process definition tools) that are used for defining and modeling the business processes and their constituent tasks. A process definition consists of a process name (e.g., purchase order process), the definition of various tasks within the process (e.g., purchase order approval task), and a set of business rules associated with the process (e.g., task sequence or data flow among tasks). The run-time component of a WFMS (also called a *workflow engine*) consists of a set of servers that interpret the process definition and create and maintain process instances. Task instances associated with each process instance are also created (based on process definition). The list of instantiated tasks pending to be executed is presented to the user (for his or her action) through a worklist server. The tasks themselves are executed in task servers. Data servers act as repositories of data that are needed by tasks. In addition, there are monitor servers that maintain the execution history for various process or task instances to facilitate run-time access control decisions.

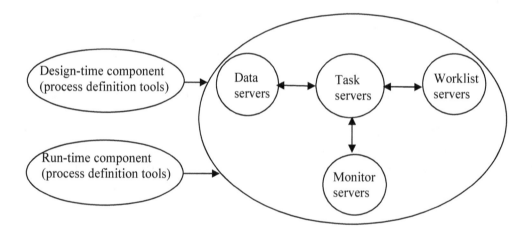

Figure 1 - Components of the Workflow Management System

The goal of the Workflow policy is to maintain consistency between the internal data and external (users') expectations of that data. Note that many individual process instances may be operational during process enactment; each needs to be associated with a specific set of data relevant to that individual process instance [WFMC99].

Chinese Wall

Brewer and Nash identified the Chinese Wall policy [BN89] to address conflict-of-interest issues related to consulting activities within banking and other financial disciplines. Like WFMS, the Chinese Wall policy is application-specific in that it applies to a narrow set of activities that are tied to specific business transactions. For example, consultants naturally are given access to proprietary information to provide a service for their clients. When a consultant gains knowledge amounting to insider information, that knowledge can be used outside the company, thus undermining the competitive advantage of one or both institutions, or used for personal profit. The stated objective of the Chinese Wall policy is to prevent illicit flows of information that can result in conflicts of interest.

The Chinese Wall policy is a commercially inspired confidentiality policy, whereas most other commercial policies focus on integrity. The access permissions change dynamically: as a subject accesses some objects, other objects that would previously have been accessible are now denied. For example, Chinese Wall policy is used where company-sensitive information is categorized into mutually disjoint conflict-of-interest categories (COI). Each company belongs to only one COI, and each COI has two or more member companies. The membership within a COI includes like companies, whereby a consultant obtaining sensitive information regarding one company would risk a conflict of interest if he or she were to obtain sensitive information concerning another company. Several COIs may coexist. For example, COI_1 may pertain to banks, while COI_2 may pertain to energy companies. The Chinese Wall policy aims to prevent a consultant from reading information for more than one company in any given COI.

There are several observations that we can make regarding this policy with respect to read operations. First, as long as a consultant has not read information belonging to any institution, the consultant is not yet bound by the policy and is free to read any sensitive information of any institution. Note that although a consultant may be free to read sensitive information under the Chinese Wall policy, he or she may be restricted from reading sensitive information with respect to another policy, such as a MAC policy. Second, once a consultant has read sensitive information of bank A, the consultant is prohibited from reading sensitive information belonging to any other bank included in the COI of which bank A is a member. Third, all consultants are free to read all the public information of all institutions.

In the history-based access control policies, previous access events are used as one of the decision factors for the next access authorization; the policies require sophisticated historical system state control for tracking and maintaining of historical events. For example, Chinese Wall policy is simple and easy to describe; however, its implementation and deployment are less straightforward.

3   CAPABILITIES AND LIMITATIONS OF ACCESS CONTROL MECHANISMS

This section describes major access control mechanisms that support most of the popular access control policies mentioned in Section 2, as well as the limitations of the mechanisms. Note that the mechanisms discussed in this section are for standalone host systems; the mechanisms for distributed systems are covered in Section 4.

In general, access control mechanisms require that security attributes be kept for users and resources. User security attributes can consist of categories such as user identifiers, groups, and roles to which users belong, or they can include security labels reflecting the level of trust bestowed on the user. Resource attributes can take on a wide variety of forms. For example, they can consist of sensitivity labels, types, or access control lists. In determining a user's ability to perform operations on a resource, access control mechanisms compare the user's security attributes to those of the resource.

Access control checks can be determined (evaluated) based on a previously determined set of rules. For example, the security label of the user must be greater than or equal to the security label of the resource for the user to read the contents of the resource. Access control checks can also be determined based on an attribute-matching algorithm. The user may perform a read operation on a resource if the user's identity and read operation pair is included in the access control list of the resource. Other characteristics of access control mechanisms include attribute review and management capabilities. For example, can the access control system determine the permissions that are associated with a user or the users who can access a resource, or better yet, both? Who can specify permissions? Can permission specification be delegated, and if so, does delegation imply further delegation? [FKC03] Access control mechanisms are often characterized in terms of their policy support; this section presents some major access control mechanisms along with discussion of the policies they support and limitations.

Note that, to be practical, the discussions exclude the limitations for each access control mechanism and the capabilities that are beyond the intended scope of the original model—for example, the historical recording capability for ACL, or rule constraints for MAC.

3.1   Access Control List (ACL) and Limitations

Resource-oriented access controls, such as access control lists (ACLs) [Pfl97], are the most common access control mechanism in use [Bar97] and by far the most common mechanism for implementing DAC policies. An ACL is an example of a policy concept that is frequently implemented directly or as an approximation in modern operating systems [At el al97, Ben96]. An *ACL* associates the permitted operation to an object and specifies all the subjects that can access the object, along with their rights to the object. That is, each entry in the list is a pair (subject, set of rights). From another point of view, an ACL corresponds to a column of the access control matrix [Sum97]. ACLs provide a straightforward way of granting or denying access for a specified user or groups of users. Without the use of access control lists, granting access to the level of granularity of a single user can be cumbersome.

The composition of an ACL entry is as follows:

- **Tag type** specifies that the ACL entry is one of the following: the file owner, the owning group, a specific named user, a specific named group, or other (meaning all other users).
- **Qualifier field** describes the specific instance of the tag type. For specific named users and specific named groups, the qualifier field contains the userid and groupid, respectively. Qualifier fields for the owner entry and owning group entries are not relevant because this information is specified elsewhere.
- **Set of permissions** specifies the access rights such as read, write, or execute for the entry.

For example,
user:rwx (*r* is read, *w* is write, and *x* is execute)
> File owner tag (with empty qualifier) specifies the owning user has read, write, and execute permission.

user.userid:rw-
> Named user tag specifies the user *userid* (qualifier) has read and write permission.

group:r-x
> Group owner tag (with empty qualifier) specifies the owning group has read and execute permission.

group.groupid:--x
> Named group tag specifies the group *groupid* (qualifier) has execute permission.

other:r--
> Other tag (with empty qualifier) specifies all other users (than the owning and named users and groups) have the read permission.

To determine the read, write, and execute access, the access check is performed on the ACL entries in the following algorithm:
1. If the user requesting access is the object owner, and the requested permission is granted by the ACL entry, then access is granted.
2. If the user requesting access is a named user in the ACL, and the requested permission is granted by the ACL entry, then access is granted.
3. If the user requesting access is in the owning group of the file, or is a member of any named groups, and the requested access permission is granted by the ACL entry of the owning group or the ACL entry of any of these named groups, then access is granted.
4. If the user requesting access is a member of any of the named groups, and the requested access permission is granted by the ACL entry of any of these named groups, then access is granted.
5. If the requested access permission is granted by the "other" entry, then access is granted, otherwise access is denied.

When a match on one of these is made, the ACL is no longer searched, and the granted or denied permissions are in effect. For example, if a user is specified as a named user, and all permissions in the entry are set to deny access to that user, the user is denied access. The groups to which the user may belong are not checked to see if the user may have access through the groups' permissions.

Table 1 is a simplified example of an ACL. In this example, a list of identifiers of the form Tag (*Group, User*) and Qualifier is used, where a * is a wildcard symbol matching any user or group name. When a user opens a file, the list is scanned and the allowed access corresponds to the first match. All groups can read *File_a*, but only group *group1* can also execute it. *Kathy* can read, write, and execute *File_b*. *Janet* has no access (-) to *File_c* unless she is in the *Group1* group. All other users have read access.

Object	
File_a	*Group.*: r; Group.group1: rx*
File_b	*User. Kathy: rwx*
File_c	*Group.group1: rx; User. Janet: - - -; *.*: r*

Table 1 – Simplified Example of an ACL

Commercial operating systems such as Microsoft (MS) Windows 2000, 2003, and XP employ ACLs for built-in access control. On an MS Windows system partition, users can set ACLs for a specific resource, such as a file or folder, by opening the Properties window from that resource's context menu and clicking on the "Security" tab. UNIX (and UNIX variants such as LINUX and FreeBSD) also support the implementation of ACLs using the baseline access control mechanism of protection bits (see Section 3.3). More details for MS Windows and UNIX (LINUX, FreeBSD) ACL implementations are listed in Appendix C.

In an ACL environment it is easy to answer the question "*who are the users that have access to this object*", but it is difficult to determine all privileges for a user, not just for that object. For instance, in such an environment one would have to search all of the ACLs. This would be all but impossible in many situations, especially for a large system where a flexible and constantly changing access control policy is required. In enterprise environments where there is significant user turnover, ACLs have serious difficulties; the sorted-order mechanism[1] of the list makes it difficult to centrally administrate ACLs, especially with a large number of users and groups. For example, if an organization decides to change from one policy model to another, it is quite likely that the new policy model will have to be implemented above the operating system level, perhaps even as part of the application code or through an intermediary. Further, different systems have their own format of ACL, which means the ACLs are platform-dependent. This is inconvenient, subject to error, slow, and makes it difficult to identify or model the overall "policy" that is enforced by the system [Hu02].

---

[1] For example, if subjects *A* and *B* both have access to object *X*, the operating system will maintain just one access list for *X*.

3.2   Protection Bits and Limitations

A protection bits (or owner/group/other) mechanism [FKC03] is commonly included in UNIX and UNIX-like operating systems. This mechanism is a simple and very common DAC control scheme that uses only a few bits of access control information attached to each file. These bits specify the defined permissions of read, write, and execute for different classes of users:

1. Owner: the file owner
2. Group: users belonging to the owner's group or project specified as the "owning group"
3. Others: the rest of the world

The access control system regulates access to a file by associating read (r), write (w), or execute (x) operations with each of these categories of users (Table 2).

Owner			Group			Other		
R	W	X	R	W	X	R	W	X

Table 2 – Permission Bits

By default, the owner of the file is the one who created the file. The owner of the file is typically the only one besides the system administrator ("superuser" or "root") who can modify the protection bits. Also note that there is only one group that is available for each file. The system administrator controls group memberships, so that as membership within these groups changes, so will the capabilities of users to access files. For example, *File_a* has the following protection bits:

File_a: (rwx) (r-x) (--x)

The protection bits indicate that the owner has read, write, and execute permission to file *File_a*; the members of the group that is associated with the owner have read and execute permission to the file; and all other system users have execute permission to the file. The "-" marking indicates that the corresponding operation is denied on *File_a*.

In general, an access control list has three mandatory entries: an owner entry, an owner group entry, and a world entry. This allows the three entries of the permission bit mechanism (owner, group, and other) to be read, write, and execute permissions at a minimum (see Table 2). Calls made to modify these ACL entries will also modify the corresponding file protection bits. Likewise, calls made to modify the file protection bits will also modify the corresponding ACL entries. This feature is intended to support backward compatibility with the large pool of existing applications that use the interfaces to the file protection bit mechanism [NSP94].

In some large systems where users are grouped by project or department, most access control needs are satisfied by a protection bits mechanism. However, this method can be cumbersome to use if permissions need to be specified for a named user who is not the owner (and nearly impossible to specify separate permissions for two users, neither of whom is the owner). It is also not possible to provide specific permissions for different named groups of users. For example, there is no way for Dave to specify that only Rick, and nobody else, should have access to a file, unless there is a group defined in the system to which only Dave and Rick belong [Gas88]. This drawback usually results in users giving world access to their files, even though they only want to make the files accessible to specific users. This limitation is likely to lead to significant vulnerabilities, because users are forced to make more and more information available to everyone. This situation violates the well-known principle of "least privilege," which states that each user should have only those permissions needed to perform his or her job, and no more. The inability to specify access rights for an individual user and specific groups pointed to the need to provide a discretionary access control mechanism that can provide the granularity of specifying individual users and named groups. For this reason, many newer versions of UNIX and UNIX-like operating systems include ACL mechanisms.

3.3   Capability List and Limitations

Another type of access control is the capability list or access list. A *capability* is a key to a specific object, along with a mode of access (read, write, or execute). In a capability system, access to an object is allowed if the subject that is requesting access possesses a capability for the object. It can thus be thought of as the inverse of an access control list: an ACL is attached to an object and specifies which subjects may access the object, while a capability list is attached to a subject and specifies which objects the subject may access. A capability is a protected identifier that both identifies the object and specifies the operations to be allowed to the user who possesses the capability. This approach corresponds to storing the access control matrix by rows. Table 3 presents an example of a capability list.

Subject	Capability	
	Object: Operations	
Ann	*File_A*: Read, Write	*File_C*: Write
Bob	*File_B*: Read	*Process_X*: Suspend
Chris	*File_B*: Execute	*File_C*: Read
Deb	*File_A*: Read	

Table 3 – Capability List

The capability list in the table is associated with a subject and specifies the subject's rights. Each entry in the list is a capability - a pair <object, set of operations>. A subject possessing a capability is proof of the subject having the access privileges. So, it can be useful to think of capabilities as being similar to tickets. However, unlike tickets, in some systems capabilities can be copied, and there may be the potential for the possessor of a capability to give a copy to someone else (this capacity is itself often represented as a "right").

A capability list corresponds to a row of the access control matrix. The principal advantage of capabilities is that it is easy to review all accesses that are authorized for a given subject. The most successful use of capabilities is at lower levels in the system, where capabilities provide the underlying protection mechanism and not the user-visible access control scheme. At the highest levels in the system, the system maintains a list of capabilities for each user. Users cannot add capabilities to this list except to cover new files that they create. Users might, however, be allowed to give access to objects by passing copies of their own capabilities to other users, and they might be able to revoke access to their own objects by taking away capabilities from others (although revocation can be difficult to implement).

Contrary to the ACL, the capability list mechanism makes it difficult to review the subjects that can access a particular object. To do so, the system would check each and every capability list for each user that may contain hundreds or thousands of entries. It is also difficult to revoke access to an object, given the need for a similar examination. For example, when an object is deleted, the system must purge capabilities for the object from every user's list. Answering a simple question such as "who has access to this object?" requires the system to undergo a long search through every user's capability list. For this reason, capability lists usually require other mechanisms to maintain the tickets. This is inconvenient, subject to error, slow, and makes it difficult to identify or model the DAC policies, and therefore is not commercially popular. At a minimum, a capability list system must ensure that capabilities are not forged or improperly changed and must control how they propagate. The advantages and disadvantages of access control lists and capability lists are summarized in Table 4.

	Access control list	Capability list
Who has access to this object?	Easy	Hard
What objects can this user access?	Hard	Easy

Table 4 – Advantages and Disadvantages of ACLs and Capability Lists

3.4 Role-Based Access Control (RBAC) and Limitations

Role-based access control (RBAC) [FKC03] policies regulate the access of users to information on the basis of the activities the users perform. Role-based policies require the identification of roles in the system. A role is a collection of permissions to use resources appropriate to a person's job function; it is thus defined as a set of actions and responsibilities associated with a particular working activity. Instead of specifying all the accesses each user is allowed to execute, access authorizations on objects are specified for roles. Users are given authorization to adopt roles.

The RBAC model taxonomy consists of four models – core RBAC, hierarchical RBAC, static constrained RBAC, and dynamic constrained RBAC. *Core RBAC* covers the basic set of features that are included in all RBAC systems. It is the inclusion of this set of features that distinguishes RBAC from other forms of authorization management systems. *Hierarchical RBAC* adds the concept of a role hierarchy, defined as a partial ordering on roles, using an inheritance relation. *Constrained RBAC* includes static and dynamic SOD (Separation of Duties) properties, which are, respectively, separation of duty rules that apply at all times, or on a session-by-session basis. *Statically constrained RBAC* adds constraint relations imposed on role assignment relations. *Dynamic constrained RBAC* imposes constraints on the activation of sets of roles that may be included as an attribute of a user's subjects. The following describe the four different types of RBAC.

3.4.1   Core

Core RBAC consist of five administrative sets: users, roles, permission, operations, and objects, where permissions are composed of operations applied to objects. The concept of role is the center of RBAC. A role is a semantic construct around which access policy is formulated. Permissions are associated with roles, and users are made members of roles, thereby acquiring the roles' permissions. A single user can be associated with one or more roles, and a single role can have one or more user members. This arrangement provides great flexibility and granularity of assignment of permissions to roles and users to roles.

3.4.2   Hierarchical

Under RBAC, roles can have overlapping responsibilities and privileges; that is, users belonging to different roles may need to perform common operations. Some general operations may be performed by all employees. In this situation, it would be inefficient and administratively cumbersome to specify repeatedly these general operations for each role that gets created. Role hierarchies can be established to provide for the natural structure of an enterprise. A role hierarchy defines roles that have unique attributes and that may contain other roles; that is, one role may implicitly include the operations that are associated with another role. For example, in the healthcare situation, a role called Specialist could contain the roles of Doctor and Intern. This means that members of the role Specialist are implicitly connected with the operations associated with their roles as Doctor and Intern without the administrator having to explicitly list the Doctor and Intern operations. Moreover, the roles Cardiologist and Rheumatologist could each contain the Specialist role. Role hierarchies are a natural way of organizing roles to reflect authority, responsibility, and competency: the role in which the user is gaining membership is not mutually exclusive with another role for which the user already possesses membership. These operations and roles can be subject to organizational policies or constraints. When operations overlap, hierarchies of roles can be established.

3.4.3   Statically Constrained

Instead of instituting costly auditing to monitor access, organizations can put constraints on access through RBAC. For example, it may seem sufficient to allow physicians to have access to all patient data records if their access is monitored carefully. With RBAC, constraints can be placed on physician access so that only those records that are associated with a particular physician can be accessed. Organizations can establish the rules for the association of operations with roles. For example, a healthcare provider may decide that the role of clinician must be constrained to post only the results of certain tests but not to distribute them where routing and human errors could violate a patient's right to privacy. Operations can also be specified in a manner that can be used in the demonstration and enforcement of laws or regulations. For example, a pharmacist can be provided with operations to dispense, but not to prescribe, medication.

An operation represents a unit of control that can be referenced by an individual role, subject to regulatory constraints within the RBAC framework. An operation can be used to capture complex security-relevant details or constraints that cannot be determined by a simple mode of access. For example, there are differences between the access needs of a teller and an accounting supervisor in a bank. The bank defines a teller role as being able to perform a savings deposit operation. This requires read and write access to specific fields within a savings file. An enterprise may also define an accounting supervisor role that is allowed to perform correction operations. These operations require read and write access to the same fields of a savings file as the teller. However, the accounting supervisor may not be allowed to initiate deposits or withdrawals but only to perform corrections after the fact. Likewise, the teller is not allowed to perform any corrections once the transaction has been completed. The difference between these two roles is the operations that are executed by the different roles and the values that are written to the transaction log file.

3.4.4 *Dynamically Constrained*

The RBAC framework provides administrators with the capability to regulate the operations that need to be performed by members of a role. Granting of user membership to roles can be limited. Some roles can be occupied only by a certain number of employees at any given period of time. The role of manager, for example, might be granted to only one employee at a time. Although an employee other than the manager may act in that role, only one person may assume the responsibilities of a manager at any given time. A user can become a new member of a role as long as the number of members allowed for the role is not exceeded.

A properly administered RBAC system enables users to carry out a broad range of authorized operations, and provides great flexibility and breadth of application. System administrators can control access at a level of abstraction that is natural to the way that enterprises typically conduct business. This is achieved by statically and dynamically regulating users' actions through the establishment and definition of roles, role hierarchies, relationships, and constraints. Thus, once an RBAC framework is established for an organization, the principal administrative actions are the granting and revoking of users into and out of roles. This is in contrast to the more conventional and less intuitive process of attempting to administer lower-level access control mechanisms directly (e.g., access control lists, access control matrices) on an object-by-object basis. Further, it is possible to associate the concept of an RBAC operation with the concept of "method" in object-oriented technology. This association leads to approaches where object-oriented technology can be used in applications and operating systems to implement an RBAC operation.

RBAC appears to fit well into the widely varying security policies of industry and government organizations. However, only a few off-the-shelf systems that implement RBAC are commercially available. Windows Server 2003 introduces a complementary authorization interface called Authorization Manager that includes role-based access control, which is based on ACLs. It explains basic concepts: roles, tasks, operations, scopes, basic application groups, and Lightweight Directory Access Protocol (LDAP) query groups. With these concepts, users can create and install authorization rules and implement the Authorization Manager application programming interface (API) [CM03]. Popular commercial database management systems such as Informix Online Dynamic Server, Oracle Enterprise Server, and Sybase Adaptive Server also provide a sound basis for implementing the basic features of RBAC, although there are significant differences among them [RS98].

3.4.5   Limitations of RBAC

RBAC assumes that all permissions needed to perform a job function can be neatly encapsulated. In fact, role engineering has turned out to be a difficult task. The challenge of RBAC is the contention between strong security and easier administration. For stronger security, it is better for each role to be more granular, thus having multiple roles per user. For easier administration, it is better to have fewer roles to manage. Organizations need to comply with privacy and other regulatory mandates and to improve enforcement of security policies while lowering overall risk and administrative costs. Meanwhile, Web-based and other types of new applications are proliferating, and the Web services application model promises to add to the complexity by weaving separate components together over the Internet to deliver application services. Moreover, the allocation of files and servers (therefore, access control) may be incompatible with organization structure (therefore, process) that requires users to focus on practical matters such as opening accounts and paying bills. RBAC products have sometimes proved challenging to implement and will, for some organizations, need to be combined with rule-based and other more time-tested access control methods to achieve the most practical value [Des03].

Although an improvement on flexibility compared to DAC and MAC, RBAC ties users to roles and associates those roles with privileges toward objects in the authorization process; it does not leave access control to the discretion of the users or roles. Therefore, RBAC is difficult to use for supporting DAC policy. It has been shown [SM02] that it is possible, though difficult, to implement DAC using RBAC by using multiple roles associated with each system object. Several variations of DAC can be supported using this method. Unfortunately, a large number of resources are required: for each object in the system, four roles and eight permissions must be created. Thus this approach to implementing DAC in RBAC is more of theoretical than practical interest. On the other hand, for real-world implementers this RBAC limitation does not present a significant problem, since most operating systems come equipped with some form of DAC, the most basic form of access control.

The least privilege condition is often difficult or costly to achieve because it is difficult to tailor access based on various attributes or constraints. A more serious concern in using RBAC is the implementation of separation of duty controls. Existing RBAC products have only rudimentary SOD features. Static SOD may be supported, but very few provide dynamic SOD. While these deficiencies may be remedied as more sophisticated products come on the market, there is a more subtle problem with using RBAC to implement SOD. With careful allocation of privileges to roles, SOD is easy and efficient to accomplish with RBAC. But if a single individual has access to all privileges needed to accomplish some critical function, then the system can be compromised regardless of the role structure. For example, suppose that two roles for initiating and approving expenditures are established with SOD between them. That is, the role that can initiate expenditures does not have the permission required to approve them, and the role for approval cannot initiate them. But if a third role is later assigned the permission to approve expenditures, and some user has access to both the initiating role and this third role, then separation of duty has been violated. In effect, a loophole has been created in the role structure. Thus, great care must be used in assigning permissions to roles to ensure that SOD requirements are not compromised. The lack of the mentioned features limits the number of policies RBAC can support. Further, RBAC is implemented under the specific access control policy, thus the flexibility is hard to support when the policy combination is required.

3.5 Rule-Based Access Control (RuBAC) and Limitations

RuBAC (as opposed to RBAC, role-based access control) allow users to access systems and information based on pre determined and configured rules. It is important to note that there is no commonly understood definition or formally defined standard for rule-based access control as there is for DAC, MAC, and RBAC. "Rule-based access" is a generic term applied to systems that allow some form of organization-defined rules, and therefore rule-based access control encompasses a broad range of systems. RuBAC may in fact be combined with other models, particularly RBAC or DAC. A RuBAC system intercepts every access request and compares the rules with the rights of the user to make an access decision. Most of the rule-based access control relies on a security label system, which dynamically composes a set of *rules* defined by a security policy. Security labels are attached to all objects, including files, directories, and devices. Sometime roles to subjects (based on their attributes) are assigned as well. RuBAC meets the business needs as well as the technical needs of controlling service access. It allows business rules to be applied to access control—for example, customers who have overdue balances may be denied service access.

As a mechanism for MAC, rules of RuBAC cannot be changed by users. The rules can be established by any attributes of a system related to the users such as domain, host, protocol, network, or IP addresses. For example, suppose that a user wants to access an object in another network on the other side of a router. The router employs RuBAC with the rule composed by the network addresses, domain, and protocol to decide whether or not the user can be granted access. If employees change their roles within the organization, their existing authentication credentials remain in effect and do not need to be re configured. Using rules in conjunction with roles adds greater flexibility because rules can be applied to people as well as to devices.

Rule-based access control can be combined with role-based access control, such that the role of a user is one of the attributes in rule setting. Some provisions of access control systems have rule-based policy engines in addition to a role-based policy engine and certain implemented dynamic policies [Des03]. For example, suppose that two of the primary types of software users are product engineers and quality engineers. Both groups usually have access to the same data, but they have different roles to perform in relation to the data and the application's function. In addition, individuals within each group have different job responsibilities that may be identified using several types of attributes such as developing programs and testing areas. Thus, the access decisions can be made in real time by a scripted policy that regulates the access between the groups of product engineers and quality engineers, and each individual within these groups. Rules can either replace or complement role-based access control. However, the creation of rules and security policies is also a complex process, so each organization will need to strike the appropriate balance.

The LINUX Rule Set Based Access Control (RSBAC) system is an open source security extension to current Linux kernels which has been continuously developed for several years.[2] The current stable version 1.2.6 was released on 7 March 2006. RSBAC was designed according to the Generalized Framework for Access Control (GFAC) to overcome the deficiencies of access control in standard Linux systems (lacking the flexible combination of security models as well as proper access logging). The RSBAC framework gives detailed access control information, and the user can implement almost any access control model in it as a runtime registered kernel module. Also, there is a powerful logging system, which makes unauthorized access attempts easily detectable. RSBAC comes with several fully functional access control modules, such as Bell-LaPadula (MAC) and ACLs. Users just have to choose which ones suit their needs best—often a combination is the best choice. The access modes are grouped into abstract request types. RSBAC provides the capability that whenever a subject wants to access an object, the respective request call with parameters request type, subject, object, and attribute data is issued. One system call can lead to several request calls (e.g., sys_open can lead to SEARCH, CREATE, TRUNCATE, and all OPEN request types).

RuBAC provides for flexibility in administrating security policies; however, it does not provide access assignments and constraints directly related between subjects, operations, and objects as other access control mechanisms do. It is the administrator's responsibility to ensure that the composing of the rules covers the necessary access constraints or permissions between subjects, operations, and objects as the policy required. Therefore, RuBAC is usually used in combination with other mechanisms. Also, because there is no formal model for rules, RuBAC may have the same limitations as other access control mechanisms do, depending upon which formal mechanism the rules of the RuBAC resemble.

3.6   XML-Based Access Control Languages and Limitations

A number of efforts have led to the development of Extensible Markup Language (XML)-based frameworks for specification of access control information. The Organization for the Advancement of Structured Information Standards' (OASIS) Extensible Access Control Markup Language (XACML) and IBM's XML Access Control Language (XACL) are access control policy specification frameworks that are mainly geared towards securing XML documents, but they can be applied to other system resources as well. Currently these languages do not provide direct support for representing traditional access controls such as DAC or MAC, but a recent extension to XACML incorporates RBAC support. Section 3.6.1 introduces XACML. Section 3.6.2 discusses using XML for policy implementation. Section 3.6.3 discusses the limitations of access control languages.

3.6.1   The Extensible Access Control Markup Language (XACML)

XACML is a general-purpose language for specifying access control policies [Pro04]. In XML terms, it defines a core schema with a namespace that can be used to express access control and authorization policies for XML objects. Since it is based on XML, it is, as its name suggests, easily extensible. XACML provides features that make it possible to support a broad range of

---

[2] More information on RSBAC is available at http://www.rsbac.org/.

policies [Oas06]; it provides the capability to request a specified action within a system using a standardized syntax, and then receive one of four replies:

- Permit – action allowed
- Deny – action disallowed
- Indeterminate – error or incorrect/missing value prevents a decision
- Not Applicable – request cannot be processed.

XACML's standardized architecture (Figure 2) for this decision-making uses two primary components: the Policy Enforcement Point (PEP) and the Policy Decision Point (PDP). The PEP constructs the request based on the user's attributes, the resource requested, the action specified, and other situation-dependent information through PIP. The PDP receives the constructed request, compares it with the applicable policy and system state through the Policy Access Point (PAP), and then returns one of the replies specified above to the PEP. The PEP then allows or denies access to the resource. The PEP and PDP components may be embedded within a single application or may be distributed across a network.

To make the PEP and PDP work, XACML provides a policy set, which is a container that holds either a policy or other policy sets, plus (possibly) links to other policies. Each individual policy is stated using a set of rules. XACML also includes methods for combining these policies and policy sets, allowing some to override others. This is necessary because the policies may overlap or conflict. Possible conflicts are resolved through policy-combining algorithms. For example, a simple policy-combining algorithm is "Deny Overrides," which causes the final decision to be Deny if any policy results in Deny. Conversely, other rules could be established to allow an action if any of a set of policies results in Allow. XACML includes standard policy-combining algorithms, and developers can create their own as well.

Determining what policy or policy set to apply is accomplished using the Target component. A target is a set of rules or conditions applied to each subject, object, and operation. When a rule's conditions are met for a subject, object, operation combination, its associated policy or policy set is applied using the process described above.

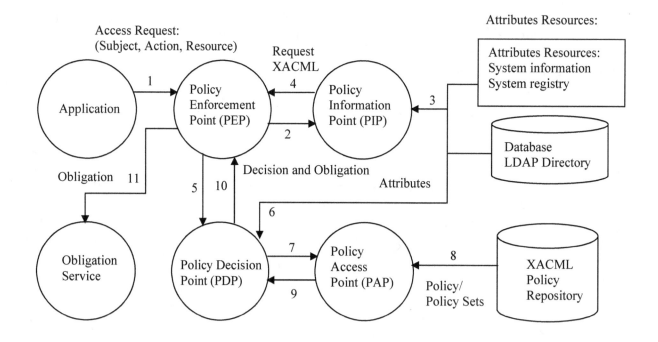

Figure 2 - XACML Architecture

Web applications can use RBAC services defined by the OASIS XACML Technical Committee.[3] The XACML specification describes building blocks from which an RBAC solution is constructed. The specification then discusses how these building blocks may be used to implement the various elements of the RBAC model.

3.6.2   Using XML for Other Access Control Models

As indicated by Ramaswamy Chandramouli of NIST in the book *Role-Based Access Control*, [FKC03] XML and XML schema specification languages gained acceptance as standards for representing, interchanging, and presenting both metadata and complex content models in a platform-independent fashion because the XML schema provides a very extensible means for specifying document structures through a comprehensive type definition language. Hence, it is the best candidate for a linguistic framework that is needed to express an access control model that embodies multiple policy requirements. The associated access control data for a given enterprise domain can then be encoded in an XML document, and the conformance of data to the enterprise access control model can be obtained by validating the XML document against the XML schema that represents the enterprise access control model through a type of software called XML parsers. These XML parsers are based on standard application programming interfaces such as Document Object Model (DOM). These parser libraries implemented in various procedural languages enable an application program written in the corresponding procedural language to create, maintain, and retrieve XML-encoded data. Hence, we have a programmable framework to extract enterprise access control data in XML documents, properly

---

[3] More information is available at http://www.oasis-open.org/committees/tc_home.php?wg_abbrev=xacml.

interpret them, and map them to the native data formats for access control mechanisms present in heterogeneous application systems within the enterprise.

Besides XML, XACML, and XACL, there are other access control languages developed in research environments, though they are not available as off-the-shelf products. Most of them have properties similar to those of the access control languages discussed here and are therefore constrained by the same limitations.

3.6.3   *Limitations of XML-Based Access Control Languages*

XML-based and other access control languages provide capabilities for composing policies from scratch, allowing users to specify a policy, together with the authorizations through the programming of the language. However, as with the RuBAC, the limitation is in the expressive power of higher-order logic such as the expressions of historical-based constraints and domain constraints.

For example, historical-based access constraint requires the manipulation and recording of access states (such as granted privileges). Most access control languages do not provide tools for the expressions of historical constraints for historical-based access control policies, thus leaving the completeness of the constraint logics to the policy writer. Domain constraints are based on the semantic information pertaining to an enterprise context; a grammar-based language cannot deal with content-based constraints. For example, an XML schema is insufficient for a complete specification of the RBAC model for an enterprise since the latter contains content-based domain constraints.   An example is not allowing more than one user to be assigned to the role of "division manager" (role cardinality constraint) and not allowing the roles "tester" and "developer" to be assigned to the same user (SOD constraint).

4   CAPABILITIES AND LIMITATIONS OF ACCESS CONTROL FOR DISTRIBUTED SYSTEMS

Determining the policy implications of a given access control mechanism is formidable. This is compounded by the wide variety of access control mechanisms used by most enterprises with distributed systems. Section 4 describes major access control mechanisms that support distributed or enterprise systems, as well as the limitations that are inherited from the mechanisms.

To provide greater policy support and control, a number of enterprise management and resource providers offer administrative capabilities over the native access control mechanisms of file management, database management, applications, and host and network operating systems. The result is an access control management system, on top of an access control management system, on top of potentially still another access control system. However, some principles, which are built on the basic access control mechanisms and often supported by a single sign-on system, are well suited for most of the distributed system environment. These principles are:

- User grouping by roles
- Access rules
- Centralized control.

Each of these principles will be demonstrated by its accompanying access control mechanisms in this section.

4.1   User Grouping by Roles

Using RBAC, an organization has central control over its resources. This is different from DAC, in which the creator of a resource determines who can access it. In most organizations, even when a resource is created by an employee, often the resource is still owned by the organization, and the organization wants some level of control over how the resource is to be shared. While the use of delegation in administration of RBAC greatly enhances flexibility and scalability, it may also reduce the control that the organization has over its resources. Because delegation of RBAC administration gives a certain degree of control to a user, that control may be only partially trusted; for some organizations, a natural security concern is whether the organization has some guarantees about who can access its resources.

For distributed systems, RBAC administrator responsibilities can be divided among central and local protection domains; that is, central protection policies can be defined at an enterprise level while leaving protection issues that are of local concern at the organizational unit level. For example, within a distributed healthcare system, operations that are associated with healthcare providers may be centrally specified and pertain to all hospitals and clinics, but the granting and revoking of memberships into specific roles may be specified by administrators at local sites.

RBAC has been implemented not only in self-contained resource management products such as DBMSs and OSs but also in a class of products called Enterprise Security Management Systems

ESMS. ESMS products are used for centralized management of authorizations for resources resident in heterogeneous systems (called target systems) distributed throughout an enterprise. In particular, an ESMS creates and manages mappings between the enterprise level (users, roles, and role membership inheritances) and the system level (user accounts, groups, and group memberships). To perform these functions, the ESMS uses agent software running on each system to create and delete groups and user accounts, populate the groups with user accounts, and set up ACLs according to commands received at the enterprise level. Groups and user IDs are central to mapping RBAC semantics at the enterprise level to permissions at the system level.

To create a mapping of an enterprise view onto a system-level group, the ESMS populates the group with the users that are assigned to and inherited by its corresponding role. In this technique, permissions are not directly assigned to roles. Permissions are assigned to groups, and groups are mapped to roles that are organized into a role hierarchy. Groups assigned to a role are included in all the roles higher up in the hierarchy. As shown in Figure 3, a graph links circled nodes of roles, groups, and non-circled users with inherited (heavy arrows), assigned (regular arrows), and group-to-role relations (dotted arrows), such that if r_1 inherits r_2, any user assigned to role r_1 becomes a member in all the groups mapped to role r_2 and by implication a member of role r_2 as well. Also, since groups are bundles of permissions as the ACL (listed in the blocked text with format of *object*: *group* (*permitted operations*), *group* (*permitted operations*)…) for each target system, permission inheritance from role r_2 also occurs. For the ESMS to grant a user membership into a local group, the user must possess an account on the system. As a consequence, for each user that is included within any group on the local system, the ESMS first creates a local user account.

Based on the concept of a sub graph, an ESMS can initially create enterprise user, role, and membership mappings to user accounts and groups. A sub graph is defined by one or more roles that are included in the role hierarchy. The sub graph corresponding to the role(s) includes the defining roles, plus any user or role that inherits the defining roles. For example, the sub graph defined by role r_1 of Figure 3 is mapped or instantiated onto Target System-1, and the sub graph defined by role r_2 is instantiated on Target System-n. Note the possibility of being able to instantiate potentially many users and roles with a single administrative operation. For example, all the users and roles within a department or division can be instantiated at one time.

The ESMS may perform this user-to-account and role-to-group(s) mapping over any number of target systems. As such, deleting a user's role assignment at the enterprise level would result in the deletion of the user's membership within multiple groups in multiple systems. But deleting a user at the enterprise level would result in the deletion of all user accounts and group memberships across all target systems where the user was instantiated. Assigning a user to a role at the enterprise level would result in the creation of user accounts and group memberships within any system for which the role assigned to the user has been previously instantiated. Using this scheme, the RBAC system can manage user IDs and groups across its scope of control through manipulating user-role assignments and role inheritance relations at the enterprise level.

Once the ESMS has created the user IDs, groups, and group memberships at the system level, local administrators may protect local resources by using user IDs and groups in expressions of local permissions.

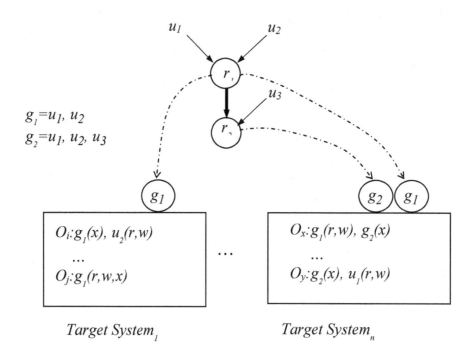

Figure 3 - Mapping RBAC for Distributed Systems

In some implementations, a user can belong only to one group. The user inherits the attributes and operations assigned to his or her group. However, in the case of conflicting settings, the settings at the user level override the settings configured at the group level. By default, users are assigned to the default group. Users who authenticate and who are not mapped to an existing group are also assigned to the default group. Alternatively, the administrator can choose not to map a user to a particular group, but rather to have the group mapped by an external authenticator. For external user databases from which the system can derive group information, it is possible to associate the group memberships defined for the users in the external user database to specific groups.

4.2 Access Rules

As mentioned in Section 3.5, RuBAC can be established by any attributes of a system related to the users such as domain, host, protocol, network, or IP address. For example, a user wants to access an object in another network on the other side of a router. The router employs RuBAC with the rule composed by the network addresses, domain, and protocol to decide whether or not the user can be granted access. So, if an employee changes his or her role within the organization, the existing authentication credentials remain in effect and do not need to be re configured. Using rules in conjunction with roles adds greater flexibility because rules can be applied to people as well as devices.

When applying RuBAC in a distributed system for access control, it is important to decide which attributes of the system to use for the rule constraints, so that there will not be conflicts in rule setting that lead to privileges leaking. Therefore, rule-based algorithms need to be devised. For example, suppose that two of the primary types of software users are product engineers and quality engineers. Both groups usually have access to the same data, but they have different roles to perform in relation to the data and the application's function. In addition, individuals within each group have different job responsibilities that may be identified using several types of attributes such as weapon programs and manufacturing areas. To avoid confusion, application-specific position codes and access profile rules are maintained for each user. When storing the data object, the data owner identifies attributes that describe the document's content and purpose. At the time of application execution, the user position codes and user's profiles are matched with document attributes to determine the user's access right.

Other example uses of the information in the directory are to make access decisions based on a person's role, or a set of rules based on any user attributes. This allows an organization to centrally control an individual's access rights to systems and information content depending on a person's role, or any other factor associated with the person, such as location, department, or language. For example, a manager in location A might need to see an entirely different set of Web resources than an account executive in location B.

4.3   Centralized Control

Many organizations with distributed systems store and manage data in centralized storage. The privileges of users for the centralized data storage access are assigned by a centralized access control system. Depending on the size and the structure of the organization, some of the access controls can be delegated to a sub level access control system, or may use a dedicated server, which is a separate system from the organization's business network. There are two commonly used techniques (systems): Centralized Object Access and Delegation of Administration Privilege, a model that was designed originally to fit into distributed network and systems. These techniques are described in Sections 4.3.1 and 4.3.2.

4.3.1   Centralized Object Access

Two popular examples of architectures for the Centralized Object Access technique are SQL and LDAP, discussed below.

SQL

Access controls have been built into popular database systems such as relational DBMSs that have been widely used in distributed systems for their flexibility and the availability of support services. Over the years, standards have been developed and are continuing to evolve. In recent years, products have incorporated a variety of access control systems. SQL[4] is the de facto standard language for defining, storing, retrieving, and manipulating data in relational DBMSs.

---

[4] SQL emerged from several projects at the IBM San Jose (now called Almaden) Research Center in the mid-1970s. Its official name now is Data Base Language SQL.

Although most relational DBMSs support some dialect of SQL, SQL compliance does not guarantee portability of a database from one DBMS to another. SQL requires certain   levels of functionality in schema specification, retrieval and modification of data, and transaction management. However, a number of security-relevant areas are not addressed. As a result, SQL-compliant DBMSs offer varying levels of security functionality. This is true because DBMS vendors typically include enhancements not required by the SQL standard but also not prohibited by it. Most products are not completely compliant with the standard. The following introduces the capabilities and concerns when using SQL to implement the three major access control policies, namely, DAC, MAC, and RBAC.

- SQL-DAC

The SQL-DAC privilege enables the creator of a relation in an SQL database to be its owner with the ability to grant other users access to that relation. The access privileges or modes recognized in SQL correspond directly to the CREATE, INSERT, SELECT, DELETE, and UPDATE SQL statements. In addition, a REFERENCES privilege controls the establishment of foreign keys to a relation. The DAC facilities are included in the current SQL standard, although the standard is incomplete and does not address several important issues. Some of these deficiencies are being addressed in the evolving standard. Different vendors have also provided more comprehensive facilities than the standard requires [NCSC96].

However, as discussed in Section 2.2.1, discretionary controls have a fundamental weakness even when access to a relation is strictly controlled. A user with SELECT access can create a copy of the relation, thereby circumventing these controls. Furthermore, even if users can be trusted not to engage deliberately in such mischief, programs replaced with Trojan horses can have the same disastrous effect. For example, in the following GRANT operation:

VINCE: GRANT SELECT ON FOR-DAVE-ONLY TO DAVE

Vince has not conferred the GRANT option on Dave. Vince's intention is that Dave should not be allowed to further grant SELECT access on FOR-DAVE-ONLY to other users. However, this intent is easily subverted as follows. Dave creates a new relation, COPY-OF-FOR-DAVE-ONLY, into which he copies all the rows of FOR-DAVE-ONLY. As the creator of COPY-OF-FOR-DAVE-ONLY, Dave can grant any privileges for it to any user. Dave can therefore grant Rick access to COPY-OF-FOR-DAVE-ONLY as follows:

DAVE: GRANT SELECT ON COPY-OF-FOR-DAVE-ONLY TO RICK

At this point, Rick has access to all the information in the original FOR-DAVE-ONLY relation. For all practical purposes, Rick has SELECT access to FOR-DAVE-ONLY, so long as Dave keeps COPY-OF-FOR-DAVE-ONLY reasonably up-to-date with respect to FOR-DAVE-ONLY.

It might be assumed that Dave is a trusted confidant of Vince and would not deliberately subvert Vince's intentions regarding the FOR-DAVE-ONLY relation. But if Dave were to use a text editor supplied by Rick, which Rick had programmed to create the COPY-OF-FOR-DAVE-

ONLY relation and execute the preceding GRANT operation, the situation might be different. Thus, a Trojan horse executed by Dave could actually grant Rick the privilege to SELECT on FOR-DAVE-ONLY. There is no way to ensure the absence of Trojan horses or other malicious code. The solution is to impose mandatory controls that cannot be violated, even by Trojan horses [SKZ03].

- SQL-MAC

MAC is not supported directly in SQL. However, there are several different methods for implementing a MAC model. Most of the methods allow users and data with different security labels to coexist. Multilevel systems implemented by these methods are said to be trusted because they keep data with different labels separated and ensure the enforcement of the simple security and strong star properties. For example, the newly emerging relational database products are basically integrated data architectures (also known as trust subject architectures). This approach requires considerable modification of existing relational DBMSs and can be supported by DBMS vendors. It should be noted that an SQL–based DBMS with mandatory access control can be designed without modification of the SQL syntax. However, certain modifications in SQL semantics must be made if polyinstantiation (there are now two records: one sensitive and one not) is used to control inference.

Security labels can be assigned to data at different levels of granularity in relational databases. Assigning labels to entire relations can be useful but is generally inconvenient. For example, if some salaries are secret but others are not, these different categories of salaries must be placed in different relations. Assigning labels to an entire column of a relation is similarly inconvenient in the general case.

The finest granularity of labeling is at the level of individual attributes of each tuple or row or at the level of individual element-level labeling. This offers considerable flexibility. Most of the products that are emerging offer labeling at the level of a tuple. Although not so flexible as element-level labeling, this approach is definitely more convenient than using relation- or column-level labels. Products in the short term can be expected to offer tuple-level labeling.

- SQL-RBAC

One of the weaknesses in early versions of SQL (ANSI SQL/89-SQL1, SQL/92-SQL2) is that they do not facilitate the management of access rights [SKZ03]. Groups of users often need similar or identical privileges, For example, all supervisors in a department might require identical privileges; similarly, all clerks might require identical privileges, different from those of the supervisors. However, with these SQL versions, each user must be explicitly granted every privilege necessary to accomplish his or her tasks. The current ANSI SQL/99 (SQL3) has included RBAC based on vendor implementations, such as in Oracle. Consensus on a standard approach to RBAC in relational databases is emerging. However, there are a number of questions that remain to be addressed before consensus on standards is achieved.

There are several mainstream commercially available products that support RBAC in some form. More than any other commercial application software, RBAC DBMSs provide access control at several levels of granularity including provision for content-dependent controls. An application system developed using a DBMS can contain a large amount of data with highly differentiated access permissions for different users depending upon their function or role with the organization. Hence, database management is a prime area that needs mechanisms for management of authorizations or privileges. Not surprisingly, DBMSs have taken the lead in providing support for RBAC.

The RBAC features that are supported have been categorized into three broad areas as follows:

- User role assignment
- Support for role relationships and constraints
- Assignable privileges.

Based on the above criteria, SQL1 is incomplete and omits revocation of privileges and control over creation of new relations and views. SQL2 fixes some of these shortcomings. However, SQL2's GRANT and REVOKE instructions apply only to database users. This is extended in SQL3 by considering that these instructions also apply to roles as suggested in the RBAC model. In the meantime, some vendors have implemented RBAC; other vendors have started to deliever products incorporating mandatory access controls for multilevel security. There is a recognition that SQL needs to evolve to take some of these developments into consideration. If it does, stronger and better access controls can be expected in future products.

LDAP

Access control for organizations with large numbers of users and distributed systems is highly complex. In one approach to dealing with the complexities of these systems, centralized Lightweight Directory Access Protocol (LDAP) directories become a major focal point as a tool for access control. The directories publishing user professional sector-related information (names, addresses, groups, roles, profiles, professional sector attributes, etc.) allow a modular, expandable access control and single sign-on (SSO) solution to be deployed rapidly for all the applications in the information system.

A major benefit of LDAP directories is the efficiency of merging groups of users under the same management system. For example, an organization wants to optimize the directories for professional sector procedures and resources common to the two groups. The concern is to optimize operating costs, and deployment should take place as quickly as possible, without changing either the administration procedures or the information processing procedures already in place. To achieve this using LDAP, the identities, roles, and professional sector attributes that were initially managed in each group's directory do not have to be imported or redefined, and the authentication and authorization policies can be managed in complete consistency, irrespective of the type of application services used.

Based on the LDAP directories, some commercial systems provide centralized and simplified user management across the distributed systems. The system ensures enforcement of assigned access policies by allowing network administrators to control (1) who can log in, (2) which privileges each user has, (3) what security audit or account billing information is recorded, and (4) which access and command controls are enabled for each configuration administrator.

4.3.2 Delegation of Administration

Kerberos is the most popular example of an architecture for the delegation of administration; it has been implemented in UNIX, UNIX-like, and Windows 2000 [Win03] and 2003 systems at the domain level.[5] Even though Kerberos is an authentication mechanism, it has been built into a system that provides network-wide security services. Kerberos can solve many of the security problems of large, distributed/heterogeneous networks, including access control and mutual authentication between clients and servers. The basic idea behind Kerberos is that a trusted third party (the Kerberos security server) provides a means by which constituents of the network (principals) can trust each other. These principals may be any hardware or software that communicates across the network.

To withstand attacks in distributed environments, a Kerberos system usually requires not only the Kerberos server but also at a minimum a Ticket Granting Service, which offers both privacy and integrity for network messages. Kerberos does not directly offer access control service, although the protocol provides for the inclusion and protection of access control information in messages for use by applications and operating systems.

When incorporated into an existing production environment, Kerberos is not transparent. Each client or application server that wants to use Kerberos services must have calls to those services included in its code. As with any other security-related coding, this "kerberization" must be based on sound application design and discipline to ensure that it is done properly.

4.4 Limitations for Distributed Systems

The same limitations of the access control mechanisms as demonstrated in Section 3 may also be applied to distributed systems, if the mechanisms are chosen for the organization. However, for different organizations and different operational environments, the impact from the limitation of the selected mechanism might not be as critical when the organization is considering the cost for the business operation.

---

[5] Kerberos is the default network authentication protocol between two Windows 2000/2003 computers if these computers are joined in a domain. Standalone systems, interactive logon, and authentication between Windows 2000/2003 and down-level clients do not use Kerberos.

5 SAFETY LIMITATIONS

Safety is an important feature of an access control systems, and is needed to ensure that the access control configuration (e.g., access control model) will not result in the leakage of permissions to an unauthorized principal. Thus, a configuration is said to be safe if no privilege can be escalated to an unauthorized or unintended principal. Safety is fundamental to ensuring that the most basic of access control policies can be enforced. However, it has been proven that the safety of an access control configuration cannot be decided for an arbitrary configuration of a general access control model, such as an access control matrix. This section consists of two subsections: Section 5.1 discusses the methods to achieve safety, and Section 5.2 covers the concept of Separation of Duty for safety.

5.1 Achieving Safety

Safety is achieved either through the use of restricted access control models that can be proven in general for that model, or via expressions called constraints that describe the safety requirements of any configuration [JT01]. Both methods are discussed in Sections 5.1.1 and 5.1.2.

5.1.1 Restricted Access Control Model for Safety

Multilevel security or separation of duty, such as MAC policy, is enforced by the safety configuration; however, a specialized model designed for a restricted or static policy is difficult to use because it is hard to ensure that the restrictions are satisfied. For example, Bell-LaPadula and Domain and Type Enforcement, which require completely trusted principals to assign subjects and objects to types (or labels), lack a simple, comprehensive approach to constraints.

5.1.2 Constraints for Safety

Constraints can be expressed in a policy that restricts access in straightforward access rules; however, creating constraint expressions for safety is a difficult task, because the entities to which safety constraints are given are not known in advance. In general, a safety constraint is expressed by a first-order predicate logic, and a few logical constraint expression languages have been proposed, but such languages are too complex for administrators to determine if a set of constraints really expresses the desired safety requirements properly. In addition, the design of higher-level expression models must be considered because approaches may be chosen that are too limited, lack necessary extensibility, and prevent administrators from understanding the relationships between constraints.

There is a trade-off between the expressive power of an access control model and the ease of safety enforcement. In a restricted model, such as Bell-LaPadula, constraints are implicit in the model's definition (e.g., a subject of one label cannot write to any object of a "lower" security label). Therefore, safety enforcement is trivial, but policy expression is limited. On the other hand, general policy expression models such as RBAC (Section 3.4) permit the definition of arbitrary constraints. In this case, the expression of safety requirements has proven to be difficult [HRU76].

5.2   Separation of Duty and Safety

In general, by restricted model, the access control policies are expressed only once by a trusted principal and fixed for the life of the system, so that access control policies are safe by definition. Currently, almost all safety-critical systems (such as military systems) use restricted access control models, such as Bell-LaPadula [Pfl97] or Domain and Type Enforcement [BSS95], because constraint expression languages are far too complex for typical administrators to use properly. However, flexibility that may be added to these models introduces the possibility of safety problems. For example, an organization uses the Bell-LaPadula model to define the extent to which principals of one label may make changes to the assignment of objects and subjects to labels. Principals that are not fully trusted are created that can modify the model. But if complete trust is not practical, then there is a possibility of safety violation. Therefore, more flexible access control modeling is often necessary when more complex safety policies are required. For example, in commercial systems, some policies require that a principal's or role's right change dynamically to prevent unauthorized actions (e.g., signing a check). Thus, configuration changes are part of the application domain. In addition, the notion that an administrator may not be fully trusted is built into some access control models, such as RBAC. To enable the enforcement of safety under these conditions, some access control models include the concept of SOD [FKC93].

As a security principle, SOD has had wide application. The purpose of SOD is to ensure that failures of omission or commission with an organization are caused only by collusion among individuals, making such failures riskier and less likely. It also minimizes chances of collusion by assigning individuals of different skills or divergent interest to separated tasks; thus, SOD is enacted whenever conflict of interest may otherwise arise in assignment of tasks within an organization. Two major types of SOD, Static and Dynamic, are discussed in Sections 5.2.1 and 5.2.2, respectively.

5.2.1   Static Separation of Duty (SSOD)

As a security mechanism, SSOD addresses two separate but related problems. Static exclusivity is the condition for which it is considered dangerous for any user to gain authorization for conflicting sets of capabilities. The motivations for exclusivity relations include, but are not limited to, reducing the likelihood of fraud or preventing the loss of user objectivity. The other problem is more of an assurance principle, dealing with the potential for collusion where the greater the number of individuals that are involved in the execution of a sensitive business function, such as purchasing an item or executing a trade, the less likely any one user will commit fraud or that any few users will collude in committing fraud.

To illustrate the value and limitations of static exclusivity constraints in enforcing separation, consider the capabilities of a cashier and a cashier supervisor, where the capability to void erroneous cashier transactions is assigned to the cashier supervisors. Clearly, a user's ability to execute the capabilities of both cashier and cashier supervisor within a single subject would constitute a conflict of interest (i.e., a user acting as cashier would be able to void his or her own transactions). One prescribed approach to this security issue is to restrict any user from simultaneously obtaining membership to both cashier and cashier supervisor. However, such an approach could impose unacceptable operational restrictions (i.e., the users authorized for the role and capabilities of cashier supervisor would never be able to perform the functions of the cashier). Examples of SSOD policies are RBAC and RuBAC (Sections 3.4 and 3.5).

SOD constraints may require that two roles be mutually exclusive, because no user should have the privileges from both roles. This might be done, for example, to deny any user the ability to both enter and authorize an order for disbursement of funds. However, permission "escalation," violating SOD requirements, may occur if a third role is assigned the requisite permissions without being included in SOD constraints. A user might have one of the mutually exclusive roles, yet acquire this third role and thereby gain the ability to violate the requirement that no individual can both enter and authorize funds disbursement. In an environment where there are numerous users, attributes, objects, and relations, safety needs to be carefully considered.

5.2.2 Dynamic Separation of Duty (DSOD)

Separation of duties can be enforced dynamically (i.e., at access time), and the decision to grant access refers to the past access history. For example, a user may be allowed to be a member of more than one user group, but to prevent conflict of interest, some policies mutually exclude user groups from being assigned to the same user. A person could be both a cashier and an accountant for a company, but only one and not both of the roles can be activated as the user performs a job-related responsibility or function.

There are various types of DSOD, such as two-person rule; the first user to execute a two-person operation can be any authorized user, whereas the second user can be any authorized user different from the first [SS94]. Another important type of DSOD is a history-based SOD that regulates, for example, that the same subject (role) cannot access the same object for variable number of times. Popular DSOD policies are the Workflow policies and Chinese Wall, as explained in Section 2.2.2.3.

6   QUALITY METRIC FOR ACCESS CONTROL SYSTEMS

Access control systems come with a wide variety of features and administrative capabilities. Some capabilities are packaged as part of an overall product offering, and others are provided as add-on features for managing access configurations within or across architectural abstractions. Although the particular access control mechanism that is included within an application or operating system is rarely scrutinized by an organization in selecting an application, its operational impact can be significant, affecting administrative and user productivity and even the organization's ability to perform its mission. Even for medium-sized enterprises, the number of users can be significant, the number of systems that need to be configured for access control can be in the hundreds, and the number of resources that need to be protected can be in the tens of millions. If a single permission is incorrectly configured, a user will either be ineffective in performing his/her duties or will be given access to unintended information and systems, which could result in undermining the security posture of the organization.

The quality of administrative capabilities has an impact on administrative cost, user downtime between administrative events, and the abilities of users to perform their duties, as well as the overall security posture of the enterprise. This section presents a quality metric for access control systems based on the configurable features and limitations of the implemented mechanism. More works need to be done for applying the metric to any specific access control systems; however, the metric can be used when considering and comparing the properties for current configuration with future expansion of an access control system.

6.1   Quality Metrics

The ability of an organization to enforce its access policies determines the degree to which its volumes of data may be protected and shared among its user community. Whether in regard to the government's war on terror or a company's formation of a strategic partnership, the focus on sharing and protecting information is becoming increasingly acute. Unfortunately, when it comes to access control mechanisms, one size does not fit all.

Access control mechanisms come in a wide variety of forms, each with their individual (and often proprietary) attributes, functions, and methods for configuring policy, and with a tight coupling to a class of policies. Instead of being individually managed, permissions of practical access control mechanisms are organized in terms of, and derived from, a set of policy-specific user attributes, providing a strategy for organizing, managing, and reviewing permission data, and controlling the access requests of subjects. The attributes of users and objects are established through administrative or system assignments. Regarding their mappings to permissions, user attributes in one form or another are associated (by rules or administrative assignments) with a defined set of capabilities. Therefore, assigning a user to an attribute indirectly associates the user with the capabilities of the attribute.

Currently there is no well-accepted metric for measuring the effectiveness or functional quality of an access control system. In consideration of the access control impacts described above and the access control primitives described in the preceding section, the following metrics are proposed:

6.1.1   The steps required for assigning and dis-assigning user capabilities into the system

For example, in RBAC, individual capabilities are assigned to a role and users are made members of that role, thereby acquiring the role's capabilities. Roles are globally created for various job functions in an organization, and users are assigned roles based on their responsibilities and qualifications. Users can be granted new capabilities as new applications and systems are incorporated, and capabilities can be easily revoked from roles (and as such revoked from users) as needed. If a user moves to a new function in the organization, the user can simply be assigned to the new role(s) corresponding to the function and removed from old roles, whereas in the absence of the role abstraction (e.g., identity-based access control), the user's old capabilities would need to be identified locally and revoked, and new capabilities would have to be granted. Although RBAC offers administrative benefits in assigning and revoking users and capabilities, RBAC would not measure as well as other mechanisms in assigning and revoking access control entries to and from objects.

6.1.2   The steps required for assigning and dis-assigning object access control entries into the system

As with user assignments, the objects can be assigned to object groups that might be arranged by secrecy levels of the objects (as in the multilevel security policy). The object groups can also be organized according to the business function; thus, the assigning/dis-assigning operations are in line with the secrecy or business functions of the organization.

6.1.3   The degree to which an access control system supports the concept of least privilege

In addition to an access control mechanism's reference mediation function, there are two other basic functions: a function to create subjects and associate these subjects with their users, and a function to associate a subject with a subset of attributes that are assigned to its user. Regardless of its implementation and the type of attributes that are deployed, reference mediation of an access control system constrains the subject and user's requests to the capabilities that are associated with a subject's attributes. Although a number of access control mechanisms associate a subject with each and every user attribute, in order for an access control mechanism to support the principle of least privilege, constraints must be placed on the attributes that are associated with a subject to further reduce the permissible capabilities. The organization-specific least-privilege policy is described by specifying the rules composed by the basic access control elements: subjects, operations, and objects. The access control systems provide various specifying methods, which achieve different degrees of granularity, flexibility, and scope, and different groupings of the controlled resources for the least-privilege policies.

6.1.4   Support for separation of duty

One of the most basic access control policies is to prevent information from unintended accesses such that object accesses are only permitted to the subjects that are duty-related to the objects (as described in Section 5). Or, in some business environments, accesses of an organization's resources are controlled to avoid conflict of interests. Such control requires limiting the object accesses to a limited number of subjects. SOD policies have had wide application in business, industry, and government. They include three basic policy types: Static Separation of Duty (for example, RBAC), Dynamic Separation of Duty (for example, Chinese Wall Policy), and Historical Separation of Duty (for example, Clark-Wilson). Different access control mechanisms provide different degrees of support for the requirement of SOD. In general, access control mechanisms allow the attributes assignment of subjects or objects that are more flexible and efficient in supporting SOD than those that do not have the attributes assignment functions. The SOD feature can be measured by counting the number of different types of SOD (such as static SOD, dynamic SOD, and historical SOD) a system can support, as well as the required steps to separate group A and B users from the group X and Y objects.

6.1.5   *Number of relationships required to create an access control policy*

Access control policies consist of a number of access control rules. Each rule is a logical expression of the basic access control elements: subjects, operations, and objects. Access control rules are composed through the user interface provided by a mechanism such as access control languages or interactive graphic tools. The interfaces may be efficient in describing particular kinds of policies while clumsy in describing others when the number of relations required to create access control rules are compared for the policies. For example, some mechanisms allow inheritance of access privileges; if user x is assigned to user group A, which inherits access privileges from group B, then x automatically inherits all the privileges of B. The only required relation for this inheritance assignment is the assigned relation of x and A. Other mechanisms without the semantic of A to B inheritance may be required to specify the additional relationship of x and B.

6.1.6   *The degree to which an access control system is adaptable to the implementation and evolution of access control policies*

Access control policies can be as diverse as the applications that rely upon them, and are heavily dependent on the needs of a particular environment. For instance, the mandatory labeling policy for the military, the commercial integrity policy for banking, and the confidentiality policy for healthcare institutions have each modeled their unique policies to meet their own internal control needs and external regulatory requirements. Although these tailored policy models are successful in the specific situations for which they were developed, notations that easily express one collection of access control policies may be awkward (or incapable) in another venue. An example of this situation would be when a company's documents are under MAC policy control at the development stage. When the development is finished, the documents that are available for use by employees could then be required to be controlled by a role-based policy. Most existing commercial technologies used to provide security to systems are restricted to a single policy model, rather than permitting a variety of models to be used. For instance, Linux applies a DAC policy, and it is difficult to implement RBAC policy (among others) in such a system. An access control mechanism that supports the implementing and evolving of policies (combining a policy with a new one or extending the current policy model) can be evaluated by the degree or the number of different well-known policies the mechanism can implement or evolves, such as the support of most of the commonly implemented policies like DAC, MAC, and Chinese Wall [SA99].

Another point of view for adaptability is to consider a computer system abstractly as a state machine performing state transitions, such that a system is considered flexible if the security policy can interpose atomically on any operation performed by the system, allowing the operation to proceed, denying the operation, or even injecting operations of its own. In such a system, the access request decision of the security policy relies on the knowledge of the entire current system state, which includes the history of the system. Because it is possible to interpose on all access requests, it is possible to modify the existing security policy and to revoke any previously granted access. The suggested approach for the needed flexibility is to identify the system state that is potentially security-relevant and to control operations that affect or are affected by that state. The degree of flexibility in such a system will depend upon the completeness of both the set of controlled operations and the current system state that is available to the security policy, as well as the granularity of the controlled operations. These factors affect the degree of flexibility because they impact the level of granularity at which sharing can be controlled.

6.1.7   The horizontal scope (across platforms and applications) of control in which users and resources are regulated under an access control policy

Depending on the architecture design, the operational coverage of an access control mechanism may be limited to the scope of platforms, applications, or enterprise environments. Example scopes are single host (as are most of the current systems), distributed network, or virtual community such as grid system. Consideration for this feature also applies if the covered scope is under the same access control policy or multiple access control policies for each system unit that can be incorporated into single access control management.

6.1.8   The vertical scope (between application, DBMS, and OS) of control

The regulation scope of an access control mechanism may be extended from the core OS to the higher system layers; then the extension can be configured through API to incorporate the existing access controls of applications, DBMSs, networks, etc. For example, an existing RBAC of the DBMS is integrated with the Chinese Wall policy such that a user has to be authorized under Chinese Wall policy first, then according to the user's role to access the database. The vertical scope of control is evaluated by the number of applications, DBMSs, and networks the mechanism is able to integrate.

6.1.9   Support for safety

One of the major issues of access control is safety (as described in Section 5). The capability of safety enforcement of an access control mechanism can be measured by the number of different types of safety constraints (restrict model or constraint expression such as different types of SOD) a mechanism can support, as well as how many operational steps are required to build a particular kind of safety constraint.

6.1.10 The degree of freedoms for AC management

Some access control systems allow the access control administrators to view and manage the access control systems by specific centric points of views from one of the subjects, operations, objects, or attributes relation mappings. For example, the administrator can view which users have read access to the objects or which objects the user can read. Some mechanisms only allow some but not all of the subject/operation/object/attribute mappings. In most cases, the display feature of a system is related to the efficiency of the access control management, because the access control display scheme was built upon the data structures that are used by the management of access control.

6.1.11 Performance of AC enforcement

The performance of access control enforcement includes the number of operations required for an access control system to grant a user's access request and for the system to check the safety (if available) of an access request. The measurement can be achieved by the computational complexities calculation according to the system model. Note that performance measures are only critical for a system that hosts a large number of users. Administrators should evaluate the number of users in the worst case to decide if performance needs to be considered [HKF06].

6.1.12 Policy conflicts that the access control system can resolve or prevent

Policy conflict appears when the specifications of two or more access rules result in the conflict decision of granting a user's access request by either direct or indirect access assignments. Policy conflict can also be a result of the deadlock of access rules specification. Deadlock can be defined as: a *rule r* has a dependency on other *rule(s)*, which eventually depend back on *r* itself such that the user's request will never reach a decision because of the cyclic referencing.

6.1.13 Flexibilities of configuration into existing systems: microkernel, application, or client/server

A microkernel is an approach to operating system design emphasizing small modules that implement the basic features of the system kernel and that are flexibly configured. The access control mechanism using a microkernel-based approach impacts the performance of a system; it has cleaner separation of mechanism and policy specified in the security architecture, enabling a richer set of security policies to be supported, but switching from one policy to another is not an easy task. Access control mechanism as an application has the advantages of flexibility and ease of installation and uninstallation; however, the access control mechanism suffers from lack of reliability caused by compromising of attacks like most of the applications. Client/server configuration of an access control system is more flexible and secure when compared with the application type of configuration; however, it requires extra hardware and thus management costs, which include the system communication overhead between clients and server.

6.1.14 Capabilities of policy encapsulation for policy combination, composition, and constraint

As described previously, access control policies may be implemented as an application, which allows the implementation by the methods of combination, composition, and constraint (Section 3.6) of different access control rules. In addition to the basic operations, an access control system might analyze the semantic or grammatical expression of access control rules and generate a new rule that encapsulates the results of the combination, composition, and constraints logics.

6.2   Metric Element Selection

As access control policies reflect the operation requirements of an organization, the quality metric should be evaluated based on the specific needs for the access control policies. For example, for policies that regulate only one host, the element of horizontal scope (Section 6.1.7) should be excluded from the metric for evaluation. Or, when only one kind of access control policy will be applied for the organization, then the adaptability to the implementation and evolution (Section 6.1.6) should not be in consideration. When multiple metric elements are selected for evaluation, one should weigh each of the elements based on the criticality for the organization's mission.

7   CONCLUSION

Although only the most commonly used access mechanisms are discussed in this document, many extensions, combinations, and different mechanisms are possible. Trade-offs and limitations are involved with all mechanisms and access control designs, so it is the user's responsibility to determine the best-fit access control mechanisms that work for their business functions and requirements.

Also included in this document are the most commonly used access control policies. Since access control policies are targeted to specific access control requirements, unlike access control mechanisms, specific limitations cannot be inherently associated with them. And like access control mechanisms, it is up to the users to select the best policies for their needs.

The complex issues of safety and the principles to achieve it are discussed. Although safety has been theoretically proven hard (non-tractable computation time) [HRU76], there are easy (practical) means to meet the requirement by providing some invariants that are not limited by the general access control model.

In addition to the limitations and issues, a quality metric depends not only on the consideration of administration cost, but also on the flexibility of the mechanism helping the user in assessing or selecting among access control systems.

APPENDIX A - GLOSSARY

Access Control

Procedures and controls that limit or detect access to critical information resources. This can be accomplished through software, biometrics devices, or physical access to a controlled space.

Access Control Matrix

A table in which each row represents a subject, each column represents an object, and each entry is the set of access rights for that subject to that object.

Access Control Policy

The set of rules that define the conditions under which an access may take place.

Assurance

The grounds for confidence that an entity meets its security objectives.

Audit

The independent examination of records and activities to ensure compliance with established controls, policy, and operational procedures and to recommend any indicated changes in controls, policy, or procedures.

Audit Trail

A chronological record of system activities that is sufficient to enable the reconstruction and examination of the sequence of events and activities surrounding or leading to an operation, procedure, or event in a security-relevant transaction from inception to results.

Authentication

Verifying the identity of a user, process, or device, often as a prerequisite to allowing access to resources in a system.

Authorization

The granting or denying of access rights to a user, program, or process.

Authorized

A system entity or actor that has been granted the right, permission, or capability to access a system resource. See also "*Authorization*".

Biometrics

The science and technology of measuring and statistically analyzing biological data. In information technology, biometrics usually refers to automated technologies for authenticating and verifying human body characteristics such as fingerprints, eye retinas and irises, voice patterns, facial patterns, and hand measurements.

Capability List
> A list attached to a subject ID specifying what accesses are allowed to the subject.

Ciphertext
> Encrypted data.

Confidentiality
> Assurance that information is not disclosed to unauthorized persons, processes, or devices. Confidentiality covers data in storage, during processing, and in transit.

Cryptography
> The art and science of using mathematics to secure information and create a high degree of trust in the electronic realm.

Decryption
> The process of changing ciphertext into plaintext.

Digital Signature
> The result of a cryptographic transformation of data that, when properly implemented, provides the services of origin authentication, data integrity, and signer nonrepudiation.

Extensible Access Control Markup Language (XACML)
> A general purpose language for specifying access control policies.

Firewall
> A system designed to prevent unauthorized accesses to or from a private network. Often used to prevent Internet users from accessing private networks connected to the Internet.

Integrity
> Preservation of the original quality and accuracy of data in written or electronic form.

Internet Protocol Security (IPsec)
> A protocol that adds security features to the standard IP protocol to provide confidentiality and integrity services.

Object
> A passive entity that contains or receives information.

Operation
> An active process invoked by a subject.

Permission (or privilege)
> Authorization to perform some action on a system.

Protection Bits

A mechanism commonly included in UNIX and UNIX-like systems that controls access based on bits specifying read, write, or execute permissions for a file's (or directory's) owner, group, or other(world).

Protocol

A set of rules (i.e., formats and procedures) for communications that computers use when sending signals between themselves.

Role

A collection of permissions in role-based access control, usually associated with a role or position within an organization.

Security Policy

The statement of required protection for the information objects.

Vulnerability

A weakness in system security procedures, hardware, design, implementation, internal controls, technical controls, physical controls, or other controls that could be accidentally triggered or intentionally exploited and result in a violation of the system's security policy.

Workflow Management System (WFMS)

A computerized information system that is responsible for scheduling and synchronizing the various tasks within the workflow, in accordance with specified task dependencies, and for sending each task to the respective processing entity (e.g., Web server or database server). The data resources that a task uses are called work items.

APPENDIX B - ACRONYMS

ACL	Access Control List
ANSI	American National Standards Institute
API	Application Programming Interface
ATM	Automated Teller Machine
COI	Conflict-of-Interest
DAC	Discretionary Access Control
DBMS	Database Management System
DOM	Document Object Model
DSOD	Dynamic Separation of Duty
ESMS	Enterprise Security Management System
FISMA	Federal Information Security Management Act
GFAC	Generalized Framework for Access Control
IP	Internet Protocol
IPsec	Internet Protocol Security
IT	Information Technology
ITL	Information Technology Laboratory
LDAP	Lightweight Directory Access Protocol
MAC	Mandatory Access Control
MS	Microsoft
NDAC	Non-Discretionary Access Control
NIST	National Institute of Standards and Technology
NISTIR	National Institute of Standards and Technology Interagency Report
OASIS	Organization for the Advancement of Structured Information Standards
OMB	Office of Management and Budget
PAP	Policy Access Point
PDP	Policy Decision Point
PEP	Policy Enforcement Point
PIN	Personal Identification Number
PIP	Policy Information Point
RBAC	Role-Based Access Control
RSBAC	Rule Set-Based Access Control

RuBAC	Rule-Based Access Control
SOD	Separation of Duty
SQL	Structured Query Language
SSO	Single Sign-On
SSOD	Static Separation of Duty
WFMC	Workflow Management Coalition
WFMS	Workflow Management System
XACL	XML Access Control Language
XACML	Extensible Access Control Markup Language
XML	Extensible Markup Language

APPENDIX C - COMMERCIAL ACCESS CONTROL SYSTEMS

System/ Access Control	Policy	Mechanism	Software
Windows Server 2003	RBAC	ACL, Active Directory, Capability List	Authorization Manager
Windows XP Professional	DAC security groups	ACL, Active Directory, Security Groups, Group Policy	Microsoft Management Console snap-ins
Windows 2000 Professional, Server	DAC, RBAC	ACL , Active Directory Group Policy Object (GPO)	Group Policy snap-in
Windows NT 4.0	DAC	ACL	Server Manager
Windows 95, 98, 98 Second Edition (SE), Millennium Edition (ME)	None (Simple File Sharing)	ACL	N/A
UNIX	DAC	ACL	UNIX Kernel
Linux	DAC, Rule-based AC	ACL	RSBAC version 0.9 for Linux kernel 2.0, 3.0 1998
SQL-compliant DBMS	RBAC, DAC, MAC	DBMS	Recent versions of Informix Online Dynamic Server Version 7.2, Oracle Enterprise Server Version 8.0 and Sybase Adaptive Server Release 11.5

REFERENCES

[AH96] Atluri V., Huang W., "An Authorization Model for Workflows," *Proceedings of the Fifth European Symposium on Research in Computer Security in Lecture Notes in Computer Science, No 1146*, 1996.

[At et al97] Atkins D., Buis P., Hare C., Kelley R., Nachenberg C., Nelson A. B., Phillips P., Ritchey T., Sheldon T., and Snyder J., "Internet Security Professional Reference," Second Edition, page 668, *New Riders Publishing*, Indianapolis, IN, 1997.

[Bar97] Barkley J., "Comparing Simple Role Based Access Control Models and Access Control Lists," *Proceeding Second ACM Workshop on Role-Based Access Control*, page 127-132, 1997.

[Ben96] Bentson R., "Inside LINUX: A Look at Operating System Development," pages 99-101, Specialized Systems Consultants, Inc., PO Box 55549 Seattle, WA 98155-0549, February 1996.

[BN89] Brewer D., and Nash M., "The Chinese Wall Security Policy," *Proc IEEE Symp Security & Privacy, IEEE Comp Soc Press,* pages 206-214, 1989.

[BSS95] Badger, L., Sterne, D. F., Sherman, D. L., Walker, K. M., Haghighat, S. A., "Practical Domain and Type Enforcement for UNIX," *IEEE Symposium on Security and Privacy*, 1995.

[CM03] Cavale M., and McPherson D., "Role-Based Access Control Using Windows Server 2003 Authorization Manager," "Role-Based Access Control for Multi-tier Applications Using Authorization Manager", Microsoft Corporation. *http://www.microsoft.com/technet*.

[Des03] Desmond J., "Roles or Rules: The Access Control Debate," *http://www.esecurityplanet.com/views/article.php/2241671*, July 29, 2003.

[FKC03] Ferraiolo D., Kuhn D., and Chandramouli R., "Role-Based Access Control," *Artech House, Computer Security Series*, 2003.

[Gas88] Gasser M., "Building A Secure Computer System," Van Nostrand Reinhold Publication, 1988.

[HFF01] Hu V., Frincke D., and Ferraiolo D., "The Policy Machine For Security Policy Management," *Proceedings ICCS Conference*, San Francisco, May 2001.

[HKF06] Hu V., Kuhn D. R., and Ferraiolo D., "The Computational Complexity of Enforceability Validation for Generic Access Control Rules," *Proceedings IEEE SUTC2006 Conference*, Taichung, Taiwan 2006.

[HRU76] Harrison M. A., Ruzzo W. L., and Ullman J. D., "Protection in Operating Systems," *Communications of the ACM, Volume 19,* 1976.

[Hu02] Hu V., "The Policy Machine For Universal Access Control," *Doctoral Dissertation*, University of Idaho, May 23, 2002.

[JT01] Jaeger T., and Tidswell J. E., "Practical Safety in Flexible Access Control Models," *ACM Transactions on Information and System Security*, Vol. 4, No. 2, May 2001, pages 158-190.

[NCSC87] National Computer Security Center (NCSC), "A Guide to Understanding Discretionary Access Control in Trusted System," *Report NSCD-TG-003 Version1*, 30 September 1987.

[NCSC88] National Computer Security Center (NCSC), "Glossary of Computer Security Terms," *Report NSCD-TG-004*, Fort Meade, Md.: NCSC, 1988.

[NCSC91] National Computer Security Center, "Integrity in Automated information System," *C Technical Report 79-91, Library No. S237, 254*, September 1991.

[NCSC96] "Trusted Database Management System Interpretation of the Trusted Computer System Evaluation Criteria," *NCSC TECHNICAL REPORT – 005 Volume 5/5 Library No. S-243,039*, 1996, http://www.radium.ncsc.mil/tpep/library/rainbow/NCSC-TR-005-5.pdf.

[NSP94] *NIST Special Publication 800-7*, National Institute of Standards and Technology, October 1994.

[Pfl97] Pfleeger C. P., "Security In Computing," Second Edition, *Prentice-Hall PTR*, 1997.

[Oas06] OASIS, "eXtensible Access Control Markup Language (XACML) TC," *http://www.oasis-open.org/committees/tc_home.php?wg_abbrev=xacml*.

[Pro04] Proctor S., "XACML: General-Purpose, Distributed Authorization," *http://kavi.oasis-open.org/archives/xacml/200403/pdf00001.pdf*, Sun Microsystems Laboratories, 2004.

[Ram02] Ramachandran J., "Designing Security Architecture Solutions," John Wiley & Sons, 2002.

[RS98] Ramaswamy C., and Sandhu R., "Role Based Access Control Features in Commercial Database Management Systems," *21st National Information Systems Security Conference*, Crystal City, Virginia, October 6-9, 1998.

[SA99] Sobel A. E. K., and Alves-Foss J., "A Trace-Based Model of the Chinese Wall Secirity Policy," page 131, Proceedings, Volume 1, *22nd National Information Systems Security Conference*, Arlington, Virginia, October 18-21, 1999.

[Shi02] Shimonski, Robert J. *Security+ Study Guide and DVD Training System*, Syngress, *2002.*

[SKZ03] Sandhu R., Kavara J., and Zorn G., "Chapter 1-2-3 Relational Data Base Access Controls Using SQL", The CISSP Open Study Guide Web Site. *http://www.cccure.org/Documents/HISM/063-065.html*.

[SM02] Sandhu. R., and Munawer Q., "Configuring Role Based Access Control to Enforce Mandatory and Discretionary Access Control Policies", *ACM Transactions on Information and System Security*, Vol. 3, No. 2, May 2002.

[SS94] Sandhu R. S., and Samarati P., "Access Control: Principles and Practice", *IEEE Communications,* Volume 32, Number 9, September 1994.

[Sum97] Summers R. C., *Secure Computing Threats and Safeguard*, McGraw-Hill, 1997.

[SZ97] Simon R.T., and Zurko M. E., "Separation of Duty in Role-Based Environments," *Proc. of the Computer Security Foundations Workshop X*, Rockport, Massachusetts, June 1997.

[WFMC99] Workflow Management Coalition, "Workflow Management Coalition Terminology & Glossary", *http://www.wfmc.org/ Documentation number WFMC-TC-1011,* February 1999.

[Win03] "Basic Overview of Kerberos User Authentication Protocol in Windows 2000", *http://support.microsoft.com/support/kb/articles/Q217/0/98.ASP*.